BE
THE
FIRST

PEOPLE OF COLOUR, IMPOSTER
SYNDROME AND THE STRUGGLE TO
SUCCEED IN A WHITE WORLD

CAROLINE FLANAGAN

www.get-known.co.u

For my boys

Dylan, Noah,
Luca and Maxwell

"

Change will not come if we wait for some other person or some other time. We are the ones we've been waiting for. We are the change that we seek.

"

– **BARACK OBAMA**

CONTENTS

PART I

YOU ARE AN IMPOSTER / 31

PART II

THE BATTLE AGAINST SYSTEMIC BIAS / 119

PART III

THE BATTLE AGAINST SELF-DOUBT / 199

THIS BOOK IS FOR

This is a book for high potential people of colour who are striving to succeed in a white world.

You know you have the potential to achieve more, but there are internal and external barriers standing in your way. These barriers create a unique form of Imposter Syndrome that has been holding you back for too long.

You are fed up of feeling excluded because of who you are and you want to be valued and included.

You are tired of being judged by the colour of your skin and you want to be recognised and respected.

You're exhausted by self-doubt and the feeling you can't compete and you want to create the results you know you're capable of.

Like me, you wish the experience of being a person of colour in a white world were different. You wish it were equal, inclusive and fair and that you could feel like you belong and can get ahead. But right now, it isn't. And as long as this continues to be the case, it's up to you to break down the barriers and do all you can to achieve the success you deserve.

This book is your call to action.

THIS BOOK WILL

This book will empower you to own your identity so you can show up as the valuable person you are. I am not here to offer you tips and tricks. This is not a quick fix. This book offers proven solutions that have worked for me and have transformed the lives and careers of my clients. In particular, the powerful tool I share in this book will:

- give you lasting confidence in who you are and the unique value you bring

- give you instant courage in the moments when you are afraid to take action

- give you a process to help you get unstuck

- motivate you to seize opportunities

- encourage you to step out of your comfort zone; and

- inspire you to achieve your potential.

I wrote this book to help you transcend the lack of diversity, inclusion and the various types of racism which are keeping you down, and to help you turn your Imposter

Syndrome to your advantage so that instead of being the barrier that holds you back, it becomes the engine that propels you forward.

As a result of doing the work recommended in this book, you will have a better relationship with yourself and you will show up to challenges differently. You'll stop feeling like a victim of circumstances waiting for an unjust system to change and so start to feel more in control. You'll feel more empowered, motivated and confident because you'll have the exact tools you need to succeed.

MEET CAROLINE FLANAGAN

Caroline Flanagan is proud to call herself an imposter. It's what generates her power and what drives her to succeed.

Against the odds, she made it from a council estate in Birmingham to being the only black student in an all-white school – twice. She went on to be one of a tiny minority of students of colour at Cambridge University, one of a sprinkling of students of colour at law school and one of the only people of colour in the room at two of the world's most prestigious law firms.

She is an international keynote speaker, certified coach, author of two books, podcast host and recognised expert on Imposter Syndrome. Caroline's mission is to help people of colour to stand out and be valued for who they are so that they can fulfil more of their potential and achieve the success they deserve.

Caroline works with some of the world's largest law firms, banks and global organisations to help support and retain their minority talent. Whether she is speaking as an expert on Imposter Syndrome on a physical stage or a virtual one, she is still often one of the only people of colour in the room.

What really lights her up is seeing the transformation her coaching clients go through as they break down the barriers they face as people of colour and achieve their potential.

Ever keen to push the boundaries of her comfort zone, she has taught sailing, bushwalking and netball in Australia; been swimming with dolphins and whale sharks; climbed mountains and trekked through the Amazon rainforest with her then 1-year-old son Noah on her back.

She never shies away from a challenge and has ice dived in Sweden, sky dived to raise money for MIND, and ran the Amsterdam half marathon to welcome her 40th with a bang and raise money for Cancer Research. In 2020, Caroline completed the navy-seals style physical endurance test known as the Goggins' challenge.

Caroline is the proud mother of four incredible boys, a fact that surprises and inspires her every single day.

Ways to connect with Caroline:

PODCAST: THE CAROLINE FLANAGAN PODCAST
HTTP://WWW.CAROLINEFLANAGAN.COM/PODCAST/

INSTAGRAM: CAROLINE_FLANAGAN_

FACEBOOK: CAROLINE.FLANAGAN.12

LINKEDIN: CAROLINE FLANAGAN

PROLOGUE

'm standing at the front of the room, and as usual, I'm feeling anxious. The room is hot and stuffy and quickly filling up with lawyers. Although I'm feeling thirsty, I can't allow myself to drink because of the adrenalin racing around my body. If I pick up a glass now the water will swirl, and everyone will see how nervous I am.

"My name is Caroline Flanagan..."

Minutes later, my nerves are forgotten, I'm feeling calmer and my talk is in full swing. I've set the stage, grabbed the audience's attention with a powerful start, and I'm at that bit in the talk where I share my story and open up my soul to the audience. I tell them all about my experience as a woman of colour making her way through a white world.

With 10 years' experience as a speaker, I've shared my story many times before. I've said, "black people" and "lady of the jungle" and "people like us"; I've talked openly about racism and prejudice and identity in front of thousands of people, but it never gets easier to stand on the stage and share your Imposter Syndrome and the moments when you've felt most alone. And each time the irony is never lost on me: nine times out of ten, I'm still one of the only black faces in the room.

I scan the audience and I'm happy to see most of them leaning forward with focused eyes, which tells me they're engaged. Some have crossed their arms, but when I make eye contact, they smile. I pause and take it all in: the size and demographic of the audience, the energy levels in the room, the inquisitive expressions on their faces while they try to deduce whether today's talk is going to be a waste of time or not. Most of them hate public speaking and wouldn't dare to stand up on stage and be in my shoes right now. But that doesn't stop them judging, having high expectations. And why shouldn't they? Time is precious after all.

I'm standing there sharing the pivotal moment in my story when, on the first day of primary school, I look around me and realise I'm the only black pupil – not in the class, but in the whole school. I want them to get the sense of how isolated I felt then, so I use the expression "one black face in a sea of white faces". It's a strong image and I do it deliberately to convey the loneliness and isolation of it all. I pause to let it sink in.

My eyes scan the room taking in all the white faces and then suddenly, they stop. There, in the third row from the back, I see a black face. It's a black face in a sea of white faces. Our eyes meet and for a minute my eye contact falters. And in that moment, I step beyond myself and the reliving of my complex story and realise that I am describing her life, the experience she is living, right now. For the white faces in the room, my story is a dramatic example of one of the many ways Imposter Syndrome can show up. But for the woman in the third row, it's not an example. It's her life.

Whenever I deliver a talk on Imposter Syndrome, whether it's to leading international firms or large global corporates, the real value that my audience gets goes beyond the deeper knowledge and understanding of what Imposter Syndrome is and how it works. It is also the discovery that Imposter Syndrome is common and the realisation that they are not alone.

If they're a white person in the audience, they get to leave the room feeling lighter, elevated by a new-found connection with those who've experienced my talk. But if they're the woman of colour in the third row, or a person like her, it's different. Yes, she may leave the room better informed, just like her white colleagues, but crucially, she doesn't get to leave the room feeling more connected and with a renewed sense of belonging. When she goes back to her desk in her top-tier law firm in the City of London, she is still the only black face. She is still alone.

INTRODUCTION

Why I wrote this book

Not enough people of colour are progressing their career or making it into leadership positions at the top. This is a problem because that's where decisions are made, cultures are created and social and economic status is gained. As long as the most lucrative and influential positions stay white, people of colour will never be equal. As a person of colour and mother of four black boys, I care deeply about this. It's why I wrote this book.

I also care that not enough people of colour are realising their potential. This matters too. To realise your potential is to bet on yourself and go all-in on what life has to offer. This involves setting ambitious goals you have no idea how to reach, heading off on the road to achieving them and rising to the challenges you'll encounter along the way – even when it's hard, even though you won't always succeed. What you get in return is the deep satisfaction of having lived life to the full, of having tested your limits and of having grown and evolved into a better version of yourself along the way. Anything short of this, and you're not fully living.

The system is broken

There are two reasons why people of colour aren't getting to the top or fulfilling their potential. The first is because of the system, which is unfair because it favours white people. There is a diversity problem, an inclusion problem and a racism problem. This system acts as an external barrier to progression that keeps people of colour down. I want to be clear that whatever you read in this book is no substitute for the urgent need for organisations and institutions to root out and eradicate the systemic bias inherent within their cultures.

The way you think about yourself is broken

The second reason is that people of colour suffer from a unique form of Imposter Syndrome that holds them back. As a person of colour striving to succeed in a white world, this is not only about the self-doubt you feel on the inside. It's about how you are treated by others as a minority, which compounds and aggravates this self-doubt. As a result, you play small, avoid opportunities that could progress your career, and you give up on hard-won careers because you don't think you have what it takes to succeed and progress any further.

"

As long as the most lucrative and influential positions stay white, people of colour will never be equal.

"

The system needs to be fixed

Of course, as people of colour, we aren't the only ones having to find ways to navigate our careers in a white world. I'm sure that if I polled the LGBT community, those of mixed abilities and the women's community, I could argue the same issues on their behalf. But there's a difference, and it's an important one: organisations have been actively pouring money, energy and resources into boosting gender diversity and LGBT diversity, and are at pains to keep track of the results. Few are showing the same commitment to racial diversity and equality and, as a result, people of colour are being left behind.

Most people accept that the system is broken and needs to be fixed. Organisations need to commit to improving diversity, making their cultures more inclusive and stamping out racism. Organisations know this, but either they aren't doing anything or they aren't doing enough. I don't need to overwhelm you with data to prove this. Take a look around you, and you'll see it. Even for the organisations who are finally showing some sort of commitment to changing things, progress is excruciatingly slow. Cultures aren't overthrown in a day.

No more waiting. It's time to step up

That's why we also need a second solution, and that is for people of colour like you to stop holding yourselves back and step up to your potential. Little is being said right now about the role that you are playing in keeping yourself stuck. At a time when the finger is being pointed at organisations and institutions that need to change, no one wants to come out and point the finger at those who have been the victims of an unjust system for generations. But I'm going to put my head above the parapet and do it. Not because we are the problem. Not because we need fixing. But because if we want things to change any time soon, we need to be part of the solution.

In 2019, I sat on the panel at an authenticity talk for the Black Solicitors Network, and I was struck by the frustration and anger felt by people of colour about their experience of striving to succeed in a white world. We discussed the micro-aggressions and the shocking examples of blatant racism people of colour are still being subjected to. Having been the only person of colour in the room for most of my childhood and throughout my professional life, I felt the same pain and hurt. I listened to how the lack of role models, the lack of inclusion and the threats to authenticity encountered by people of colour were preventing people of colour from making it to the top and it sounded all too familiar. But a part of me rebelled against the powerlessness in the room. I reflected on my journey to date, the challenges I'd faced and how I had overcome these and I felt a burning longing to talk more about where power comes from and the extraordinary results we can create when we find the power in ourselves and we use it. Toni Morrison said, "If there's a book that you want to read, but it hasn't been written yet, you must be the one to write it."

This personal empowerment book is the book I want to read when the odds are against me and I need to find a way to win. I hope this book will be the same for you.

The system needs fixing. But when we only talk about what is wrong outside of us we overlook what's going on within us. This is to our cost for two reasons:

1. We give away our power: we depend on the white majority to solve the problem and, for as long as they choose not to do this, or are slow and resistant to it, we are stuck with the way things are. We can appeal to their sense of fairness and their morals, we can try to shame and guilt them into change. But if our success depends entirely on trying to control how others behave, we'll never be free.

2. We are still left with our internal struggle: even when the system is fixed, we will still have our own

internal barriers to overcome – self-doubt, the fear of failure and the legacy of racism that makes us doubt our value and question our right to be here or reach for the top. Without the tools to overcome them, these internal barriers will continue to hold you back long after the systemic barriers to progression that you currently face fall away.

This book aims to change that. It will give you back your power so you have more control, more confidence and the motivation to stay on track so you can fulfil more of your potential, and in doing so become part of the solution.

Why you need this book

As a person of colour struggling to succeed in a white world, progressing your career can feel like a battle you can't win because so much about you is different to those who are succeeding around you. When the odds are against you like this, it's easy to think you're powerless, but you're not. This book will remind you how powerful you are and provide you with the tools to channel that power into making a difference, to yourself and to the world.

It does this first by giving you a deeper understanding of your unique form of Imposter Syndrome (Part I: You are an

Imposter). Then, it shows you how to transcend the external barriers that are holding you back (Part II: The Battle Against Systemic Bias). It will then give you a powerful practical tool that will give you instant courage and lasting confidence so you can realise your true potential (Part III: The Battle Against Self-Doubt).

A new look at Imposter Syndrome

I'll be honest, I wasn't in a hurry to write a book about Imposter Syndrome, even though it has been one of my areas of expertise for several years. There has been no shortage of books, research papers and surveys on the subject in recent years. I wasn't in a hurry to write a book about Imposter Syndrome generally that would get lost in the noise.

And then I saw your one black face in the sea of white faces, and I made the connection between the battles I have fought my whole life and the same battle you are in, and I understood how different your experience of Imposter Syndrome is to that of your white peers and colleagues. This meant that the usual solutions for coping with Imposter Syndrome which hadn't worked for me in the past, wouldn't work for you either. Like me, you need something more. Reflecting on how I've managed to achieve success as an imposter in a white world, I realised that I was uniquely positioned to provide it.

That something more is a powerful tool which I created in 2015 as a solution to my own Imposter Syndrome. That tool helped me turn my Imposter Syndrome from a weakness that was holding me back, into a strength that gave me the courage, motivation and inspiration to fulfil more of my potential. I have overcome the legacy of systemic bias and the trappings of my own self-doubt, and I've achieved more than I would have previously imagined possible. This tool has been, and continues to be, transformational for me and it can be the same for you. In this book, I'm going to show you how to create it for yourself and how to put it to use in the real world so that you too can fulfil your enormous potential.

What it means to be the first

Most people think that being the first is about being the first one to cross the finish line. Sometimes this is the case. Sometimes, like Barack Obama, Nelson Mandela, Tiger Woods, Wataru Misaka or Simone Biles, you really are the first person of colour to be promoted, hold a certain leadership position, or blaze a trail and this is an extraordinary, remarkable achievement. But being the first isn't always about being the first across the line. In this book, I'm going to show you that the final achievement is not the only way to be the first and, while it is hugely significant in many ways, it is not the most important. What is more important, and what it means to truly be the first, is to be the imposter in the room and still throw your heart and soul into trying to succeed. It's being the one who doesn't belong and who feels excluded; the one who has no role models to follow and who must constantly weigh up the opportunity to succeed and the risk to their authenticity, and for whom the path to success is so lonely at times, it feels like you're the first. Being the first means being the imposter, yet still showing up with the courage and determination to succeed. This book is an opportunity to build a stronger, more powerful identity and to leverage that identity as a tool for progressing your career and fulfilling our greatest potential.

Why "people of colour"?

When I first came up with the idea for this book, I was proud and excited to talk about what it would do for the "BAME" – Black Asian and Minority Ethnic Origin – community. Towards the end of 2019, this expression was a generally accepted term amongst my corporate clients for grouping all ethnic minorities together, in a bid to provide us with more targeted career support and professional development.

Personally, I did not find this insulting or frustrating. I have spent years studying and working in environments where the challenges of being black in a white world were never openly acknowledged. As a result, I felt genuinely excited to see our specific challenges being recognised in the corporate space as in need of special attention if we are to succeed in making it to the top. And I have been excited, through my keynote talks and executive coaching, to play my part in supporting such initiatives.

However, since then the acronym "BAME", with its implication that all ethnic minorities are the same, has provoked immense and intense frustration, and even anger. Many of you resent being grouped into one homogenous group and treated as if we are all the same. In response to this, I decided to drop all references in the book to "BAME" (except where it is part of a reference). Not because I disapprove of it, nor because I felt pressured to do so. Simply because there is an important message in this book that I want you to hear. If the expression "BAME" is a barrier that could prevent you from hearing it, I'm only too happy to let it go.

I have chosen "people of colour" instead.

Of course, some of you will hate the expression "people of colour" too! But you can't please everybody all of the time. If this is you, I invite you to read the book in the spirit in which it was intended: to empower, motivate and support you as a high potential member of a minority group to succeed against the odds, fulfil your amazing potential and be the change we want to see in the world.

Lastly, a word about names.

Throughout the book, you'll find examples and case studies relating to clients, friends, colleagues and people I've encountered along the way. Please note that unless otherwise stated and in the interests of maintaining confidentiality, I have not used their real names.

PART I

YOU ARE AN IMPOSTER

INTRODUCTION TO PART I

I n Part I, we explore the origins and symptoms of the unique form of self-doubt we call Imposter Syndrome. We'll discover who Imposter Syndrome affects, the reasons it shows up and the impact it is having on you, both personally and professionally.

Then we look at Imposter Syndrome in high potential people of colour who are striving for success in a white world. You'll discover that people of colour with Imposter Syndrome face a double challenge because they are fighting two battles, rather than one. We'll discuss the specific experiences of people of colour in the workplace, and the personal and aspirational costs that result from this.

I'll then share my personal experience of Imposter Syndrome as a person of colour who has been striving for success in a white world my whole life, and who has learned how to win. You'll learn that the barriers you face in your workplace don't have to stop you or hold you back. Although the battles you are facing are hard, they are battles you can win because you are so much more powerful than you may think.

_____

DISCOVERING YOU HAVE IMPOSTER SYNDROME

"The real voyage of discovery consists not in seeking new landscapes but in having new eyes."

– MARCEL PROUST

Welcome to Imposter Syndrome

It's happening again. Panic. Shortness of breath. There's a rock-hard knot of anxiety forming in the pit of my stomach.

When I get like this it's difficult to breathe. My palms become sweaty, my cheeks begin to burn and it feels as though the walls are closing in on me. But worse than any of this is the voice of fear and dread that whispers threateningly in my ear each and every time. Its tone may vary. The choice of words may change. But the warning is always the same: "You shouldn't be here! Don't do it! Your luck will

"

Discovering you have Imposter Syndrome is the first step to owning it.

"

run out and you'll fail. And when that happens, you'll be exposed and lose everything."

Welcome to Imposter Syndrome.

Does any of this sound familiar? Do you, like me, have an inner voice that issues terrified warnings from deep inside you when you're about to take on a challenge or you've been assigned a new task? Does your inner voice tell you that you don't deserve your success and that everyone else around you is more qualified to seize the opportunity in front of you? Do you believe you are a fraud and live in permanent fear of being found out?

If the answer to any of the above is yes, then the chances are you have Imposter Syndrome – a unique form of self-doubt which acts as a silent tormentor to a purported 75% of the population at some point in their life. If you're reading this book, I'm guessing you're one of them.

In this chapter I'm going to explain exactly what Imposter Syndrome is (and what it is not), who it affects and the havoc it is wreaking on the self-esteem, performance and mental health of high potential people just like you. I will give you a clear understanding of this fascinating phenomenon. If you're already familiar with Imposter Syndrome, it will serve as a helpful reminder. If you're new to Imposter Syndrome, it will tell you exactly what you need to know. By the end of this chapter, you'll know and understand exactly what it is so you can recognise it in yourself and contemplate the effect it may be having on your life. Discovering you have Imposter Syndrome is the first step to owning it.

I suffered from Imposter Syndrome long before I knew what it was. When I finally made the discovery, it wasn't just a relief to know it was actually a thing, it was life-changing.

DISCOVERING I'M NOT ALONE

On a bleak January morning in 2006, I dragged myself out of bed at the ungodly hour of 5.20am and crept as quietly as I could downstairs. Two-year-old Dylan and 6-month-old Noah were still fast asleep, and I was determined to keep it that way. That first peaceful hour of the day, before kids and husband and the world start demanding my attention, was (and still is) the most precious thing to me – a delightful oasis of calm when I can dedicate myself to all those things I struggled to find time for in the day: exercise, me-time, reading. On the day in question, I made it downstairs successfully, grabbed my first cup of tea of the day, my second-hand copy of *Unstoppable People* by Adrian Gilpin and snuggled into my favourite armchair.

A few minutes into reading, I suddenly sat bolt upright. I remember squinting my eyes in confusion and frowning in disbelief. I couldn't believe what I was reading. It was as if the author had looked into my soul, read my story and handed me the answer to a puzzle I'd been struggling with my whole life.

"You feel like a fraud.

You think your success is down to luck.

You fear that any minute now you'll be exposed.[1]"

Reading these words was like exhaling for the first time after years of holding my breath. I couldn't believe it. Not only did someone out there understand how I'd been feeling all these years, but there was actually a name for it:

Imposter Syndrome.

For years, anxiety, the fear of failure and what felt like an imminent threat of exposure had been hovering over me like the sword of Damocles. Being asked a question at school would provoke major internal panic and shortness of breath. Completing a piece of homework would trigger a full-blown identity crisis. Sitting exams, being asked my opinion, applying for university, jobs, training contracts; sometimes even the simple act of facing another day could cause anxiety, rocketing stress levels and a compulsive drive for perfection to avoid being found out. My whole life, up until that point, I believed it was just me. And then, suddenly and without warning, I'm sitting in an armchair at the age of 31, drinking tea and reading a book, and I discover that the fear that had haunted me all of these years is actually a thing.

Unstoppable People was an unforgettable moment. It changed everything for me because it showed me, after years of quiet suffering and inner turmoil, I wasn't alone.

You mean it's a thing?

If you've ever felt like a fraud, that your success is down to luck, and that any minute now you'll be exposed, the moment you first hear about Imposter Syndrome is a strangely beautiful thing. As a keynote speaker on this topic for over six years, I consider it a privilege to witness that moment in others. Of those who come to my talks, a surprising number have no knowledge of Imposter Syndrome. For them, the revelation that their feelings are not only valid, but common, is an astonishing one. It's a life-changing moment that brings relief and wonder and, most of all, hope. "If it's actually a thing, then maybe I'm not crazy." "If it's a thing that other people have, then I'm not alone." "If it's a real thing, a legitimate, recognised thing, then maybe there's hope." When we name something, not only do we make it real, we also create something we can talk about and start to have control over.

Origins

Of course, it's all very well putting a group of feelings together and giving them a fancy name. But if you're anything like me, you'll also want to understand it at an academic level too. *Where does it come from?* and *How do I know this thing is real?* were questions I felt compelled to answer before I could fully embrace it as an explanation of my own condition.

"An internal feeling of intellectual phoniness."

**- DR PAULINE R. CLANCE AND
DR SUZANNE A. IMES**

The discovery that the term "imposter phenomenon" (as it was first referred to) was coined as long ago as 1978 by two American psychologists, Dr Pauline R. Clance and Dr Suzanne A. Imes[2], came as a complete surprise to me. I asked myself then, as you may be asking yourself now, how come I'd never heard of it before, and why weren't more people talking about it (a question I'll come back to shortly). What I found even more fascinating was how closely my own experience mirrored that of those in whom Clance and Imes first made their discovery. They were a group of high-achieving women who, from the outside, were clearly successful and highly competent. But from the inside, these women couldn't see it. They saw themselves as intellectual frauds and lived in fear of being exposed as imposters. They believed their success was down to luck and the result of having deceived others into thinking they were cleverer or more capable than they were. As a result, they suffered from anxiety, fear of failure, low self-confidence and, in some cases, a general dissatisfaction with life. Any of this sound familiar?

What are the symptoms?

If you're still unsure about whether you suffer from Imposter Syndrome, there are streams of research that point to the easily identifiable symptoms. For me, and for many others who I've described it to for the first time, the word "fraud" sums it up perfectly. And it isn't just the feeling that you're a fraud that is so easy for us to relate to. It's the extreme lengths we go to in order to avoid being found out. Overpreparing, perfectionism and being driven by a terrorising fear of failure, are prime examples. The need to overdeliver at all times, no matter the importance of the task, is another. Just last week I delivered a keynote and Q&A session on Imposter Syndrome with a group of high-achieving women working in the construction industry. A poll showed that the percentage of people in the room who felt they suffered from Imposter Syndrome was an astonishing 99%. And every single one of them cited a compulsive need to overprepare and overdeliver as a key feature of their experience. Even worse, was the tendency to do so in secret – hiding the truth about the number of hours they actually worked in order to avoid seeming inefficient.

This overzealousness certainly produces results. Overpreparation and perfectionism often lead to success and high achievement. But the relief and reassurance that comes from these results are fleeting. Before you know it, your inner voice pipes up to tell you you're still a fraud and at risk of being found out, except that now the risk is higher because your luck is running out. The self-doubt and anxiety this provokes follow you to the next task, and the cycle continues.

Another feature of Imposter Syndrome is an inability to accept praise. If, when you receive positive feedback or clear evidence of success – your boss gives you a fantastic end of year review; you're nominated for an award; or you receive glowing feedback at the end of a successful project for example – your default response is to discount and discredit it, then this is a sure sign you have Imposter Syndrome. One of the ways you do this is by fixating on a minor error, or a piece of feedback that could be construed as negative and giving it a disproportionate amount of importance.

"Each time I write a book, every time I face that yellow pad, the challenge is so great. I have written a relevant book, but each time I think, 'Uh oh, they're going to find out now. I've run a game on everybody and they're going to find me out'."

– MAYA ANGELOU

As with the perfectionism and the overpreparation, I know this symptom all too well. Give me positive feedback, congratulate me on a success, and my instinct is to deny. Left to its own devices, my brain will get straight to work, searching for evidence of imperfection that I can use to discredit all of the good stuff that is being said. I remember early on in my speaking career, when I delivered one of my first talks on Imposter Syndrome, the written feedback was incredible. I should have been proud, delighted, jubilant at my success in keeping my nerves at bay, delivering my message and engaging the audience. I should have lapped up the superlatives and been thankful that almost everyone in the room fed back. But instead, I found the one feedback form out of over 40 forms, which contained what I perceived to be a negative comment and I allowed it to devastate me. I cried. I beat myself up. I swore I would never step on a stage to speak before an audience ever again. That's what Imposter Syndrome can do to you if you don't have the right tool to address it.

HOW TO TELL IF YOU SUFFER FROM IMPOSTER SYNDROME

According to Clance (1985), Imposter Syndrome is evident by the presence of any two of the following characteristics:

1. You overwork

The amount of effort and energy you invest in a task far exceeds what is needed to produce decent quality work. You know this, but you're so afraid of the fear of failure you can't break the cycle.

2. You need to be special, to be the best

You were typically top of the class at school. But in a larger setting, such as university or work, you realise there are many other exceptional people with talent and ability, so you dismiss your own talents as not good enough.

3. You are a perfectionist with a superwoman or superman drive

You expect to do everything perfectly in every aspect of your life. You set high and almost impossible standards and work relentlessly to try to achieve them.

4. You fear failure

You experience huge anxiety when there's a task to be done because you're so afraid of failure. If you make a mistake, you feel shame and humiliation.

5. You deny your abilities and discount praise

You discount positive feedback and ignore the evidence of your success, preferring instead to look for evidence of failure or develop arguments to prove you don't deserve praise or success.

6. You fear success, and feel guilty about it

You fear your success will have negative consequences, for example, when successes are unusual in your family or your peer group. You often feel less connected and more distant when you become successful. You may be overwhelmed by guilt about being different and worry about being rejected by others. You fear that success will lead to higher demands and greater expectations from those around you and wonder how you can maintain this level of performance. You're reluctant to accept additional responsibility as you fear that higher demands and expectations will expose you as a fraud.

Who has Imposter Syndrome?

The original research on Imposter Syndrome suggested that it was unique to women. If you were to attend my talks and open session Q&As on Imposter Syndrome you would be forgiven for jumping to that same conclusion. In fact, the most frequently asked question at these events is: do men suffer too?

The assumption often is that Imposter Syndrome is suffered by women who are disenfranchised by a white patriarchal system which rewards risk-takers, braggers and those who are innately confident. But, if you're lucky, there may be a handful of men in the room who will dissuade you of that notion. As is also made clear by the stories in this book, Imposter Syndrome is not a female phenomenon. It's a human one.

Of the thousand plus people who have attended my talks on Imposter Syndrome, the statistics are interesting. Some 40% of those who sign up to the event ahead of time and complete the pre-event survey are men. Meanwhile, 55% are women (leaving roughly 5% who didn't want to be identified by gender). However, without exception, on the day of the event, the split changes. At least 95% of those in the room are women. Men seem to have an interest in the topic beforehand, but when it comes to the live event, they don't show. There may be many reasons for this. I'd hazard a guess, which conversations with the small number of men who do show up confirm, that one of those reasons is a reluctance to talk openly about a subject that reveals our vulnerability. This is not at all surprising when you consider that the context for most of these talks until very recently, was a lunchtime session in a corporate setting surrounded by the peers, colleagues and bosses you have spent years hiding your Imposter Syndrome from. Certainly, one conclusion we can no longer draw is that Imposter Syndrome is limited to women only. My research supports this.

Sexual orientation, religion, cultures and other points of difference

Imposter Syndrome has been shown to cross not only genders, but also occupations and cultures[3]. I see this played out at my Imposter Syndrome events which are attended by people from a broad cross-section of industries and cultures – from business owners to corporate employees; from students and recently graduated employees to those at senior management and partnership level. And it isn't limited to the world of law or finance, where most of my clients work. Imposter Syndrome resonates with creatives, civil servants, doctors, people in tech and members of the police force. Imposter Syndrome is not, therefore, an exclusive condition we can attribute to a particular demographic. What all Imposter Syndrome sufferers do have in common is a real or perceived difference that separates them from the majority of those around them.

That difference is sometimes obvious. The lone woman in the boardroom full of men is one example. The only black barrister in a mostly white barristers chambers is another (I'll be exploring the specific experience of people of colour with Imposter Syndrome in the next chapter). But sometimes the difference is less visible – sexual orientation or religious persuasion, for example. If you are (or believe yourself to be) the only one from a particular socio-economic background, type of education, cultural background or physical ability, that difference you experience is fertile ground for Imposter Syndrome to take root.

What's so special about Imposter Syndrome?

Recent studies point to the notion that Imposter Syndrome affects the vast majority of people. It certainly seems to be losing its taboo status. Numerous celebrities, influencers, actors and politicians – Nicola Sturgeon, Ellie Goulding, Tom Hanks, Sheryl Sandberg, Maya Angelou and Michelle Obama to name a few – have been going public with their Imposter Syndrome. It's pretty amazing. Six years ago, when I started delivering talks on Imposter Syndrome, few people had heard of it. Now, barely a day goes by without a celebrity announcing their Imposter Syndrome, or a friend mentioning it while out for a drink, or you overhear it being discussed at a networking event. It's almost as if it's becoming cool to have Imposter Syndrome! This begs the question – if the majority of us have it from time to time, what's so special about Imposter Syndrome? Surely, it's just a fancy word for ordinary self-doubt?

It holds you hostage

MICHAEL'S STORY

Michael would disagree. Michael approached me after a talk on Imposter Syndrome at the 2016 Future Leaders Conference in London. [You can watch a clip of this event here – **https://www.youtube.com/watch?v=RXF-5Y4k4iw**]

After hearing my experience and advice on Imposter Syndrome, Michael wanted to thank me for my insights and share some of his own story. Michael is Hong Kong Chinese. He'd been top of his class all through school and had graduated from Oxford University with a first-class honours degree in Economics. He had applied for several jobs and was currently sitting on not one, not two, but three job offers to join the graduate schemes of some of the world's most prestigious organisations. And yet, Michael was miserable. The reality of this success was not a source of pride for him. Instead of giving him the reassurance and confidence to start his career, his remarkable success had left him feeling more vulnerable, anxious and exposed than ever. "I just can't escape this feeling. I'm terrified that when I start, my luck will run out and this will all come crashing down." As he described his experience, the paralysing effect of this success (he had been sitting on those offers for days and would soon run out of time to accept them) and the suffering his Imposter Syndrome was causing him, I could see real pain in his eyes. This was no ordinary form of self-doubt. His Imposter Syndrome wasn't keeping his ego in check. It was holding him hostage.

The more you achieve, the worse it gets

What's so special about Imposter Syndrome is a question that comes up in my sessions, and in the public conversation. BBC Radio host Vanessa Feltz found this to her delight when Michelle Obama confessed to suffering from Imposter Syndrome during her world tour to promote her biography, Becoming. The phone lines on Feltz's show were alight with callers keen to show their empathy with the former First Lady. There was no shortage of opinions and advice on the nature of Imposter Syndrome and how to deal with it. If this had been your first introduction to Imposter Syndrome, you'd have been left with the impression that Imposter Syndrome was just a fancy word for ordinary self-doubt, that most people get it, and that it's actually a good thing because it helps us to achieve and it keeps us humble.

"What's it called when you have a disease, and it keeps recurring? I go through [acute imposter syndrome] with every role. I think winning an Oscar may, in fact, have made it worse."

– LUPITA NYONG'O

But to reduce Imposter Syndrome to every day self-doubt is to miss the point. Imposter Syndrome is anything but ordinary. It cannot be eradicated by praise or cancelled out by achievement. That's why it's unique. The more you achieve, the worse it gets. With Imposter Syndrome, success does not mean happiness[4]. Success doesn't weaken the feeling of fraudulence, it reinforces it[5]. Unlike with ordinary self-doubt, where your confidence grows from repeated successes, success doesn't fix the problem with Imposter Syndrome. It compounds it.

It's prevalent in high achievers and has no grounding in reality

The other important distinction I make between self-doubt and Imposter Syndrome (and one of the things I find most fascinating) is how common it is in high achievers. Over-working, the need to be the best, perfectionism and a fear of failure are the exact qualities that push people to chase success and high achievement. The research will tell you it is not limited to high achievers. But what I know from personal experience, and what I have witnessed in my professional capacity as a coach and a speaker, is that competitive and demanding work cultures are a magnet for perfectionists whose high performance is driven by the fear of being a fraud.

It's hidden

Because of the achievements and success that typically surrounds someone with Imposter Syndrome, it's a condition you rarely see. If you attend one of my talks, you won't see my Imposter Syndrome. You'll have no idea how little sleep I had the night before, or that five minutes before walking on stage my heart was exploding in my chest and the voice in my head was screaming at me to run because seriously, honestly, this time my luck really will run out. You'll see none of this. By the time I step on stage, I am the picture of confidence. Thanks to years of practice, I can make it look easy. Many of you are show-ing up like this every day: calm composure on the outside masking the inner turmoil and fear on the inside.

Imposter Syndrome, by its very nature, is hidden. If you are afraid of being exposed as a fraud and you believe your success is undeserved or down to luck, the last thing you want is to be found out. There is an almost compulsive need to keep achieving in order to avoid exposure. Don't make the mistake of assuming those more senior to you, or who act more confidently than you, are immune from it. Imposter Syndrome can be found lurking beneath the surface of those who appear to be the most accomplished and successful – your boss; the loudest colleague in your office; someone you've looked up to all your life. Even if there appears to be a greater willingness to talk openly about it on the public stage, in the quiet corners and bustling corridors of high pressure, high performing, competitive corporates and law firms, individual battles with Imposter Syndrome are secretly being fought every day.

ALAN'S STORY

Take Alan, for example. Alan is a tall, weathered-looking man in a dated suit and a busy, old-school tie. He is a man with self-assured seniority etched on his face – wizened eyes, thinning hair and a permanent furrow between his brows. I spotted him at the back of the room during the pre-event reception drinks at an Imposter Syndrome talk I was delivering for a law firm client, talking to another man. It was a rainy dark wintry evening in the north of England – the kind of evening where the last thing you want to do is stay late in the office, even if it's to attend one of my events on Imposter Syndrome! There are usually more women than men at these events, so when I spotted two men in the corner of the room, it piqued my interest. I headed straight for them.

I love meeting members of the audience before a talk to learn more about them and find out why they've come. When I asked Alan what had attracted him to the event, he was quick to correct me. "Oh no, I'm not here for you," he said, "I'm here for my client. I'm not interested in Imposter Syndrome at all. I'll be at the back. Just ignore me," he said. I half-joked about getting him involved and asking him questions, but his response was deadly serious: "I'm not interested in this at all," he said. "I'll be at the back by the door. Leave me out of it."

One thing you should know about me when you attend my events is, I like to get people talking. My aim is to create an environment where everyone in the room feels it's safe to share and is willing to engage. When an audience willingly participates in the conversation and wants to delve deeper into the issues, I know I've done my job. So when someone like Alan asks me to leave him out of it, I aim to find a way to respectfully include him. But his message that day was unequivocal. So I decided to leave him to it.

Which is why it was no surprise to me when, halfway through my talk, I saw Alan get up from his seat and leave the room. Of course, I thought. He's shown his face and now he's leaving. I felt a momentary pang of regret that my talk had failed to reach him but continued as if nothing had happened. Five minutes later, the door opens and, to my surprise, Alan heads back to his seat.

During the reception drinks afterwards, with the buzz and excitement and energy from the session still filling the air, I look across the room and see Alan. Not only is he still here, I think, but he's also one of the last to leave. I head straight for him. The conversation that followed was one of the reasons why exploring Imposter Syndrome in high-performing environments is so important. Alan told me he'd only attended the event to show his face to the client, and planned to leave after 10 minutes, but he'd found himself unable to "because" he said, "at a certain point, it felt like you were talking directly to me. I realised for the first time, at the age of 58, that I've suffered from Imposter Syndrome my whole life".

As well as being a profound moment (this is the kind of magical transformation every inspirational speaker

"

*Imposter
Syndrome cannot
be eradicated
by praise or
cancelled out by
achievement.*

"

dreams of igniting in their audience), this was an incredible example of how deeply embedded and heavily disguised Imposter Syndrome can be. If you know you suffer from Imposter Syndrome, and you're feeling like the only one, always remember this: there are imposters all around you. You're not alone.

IMPOSTER SYNDROME MYTHS

- It only affects women. Men don't suffer

- It's a healthy form of self-doubt

- It keeps you humble

- Everyone has Imposter Syndrome

- It's worse for young people (who lack the confidence that comes with experience)

- It's worse for older people (who aren't as quick and innovative as the young)

- It's a gender thing

- It's an ethnicity thing

- It's a religion thing

What impact does it have?

If Imposter Syndrome goes hand in hand with high achievement, what's all the fuss about? If you're still able to do your job and succeed, why should anyone care?

When you consider someone like Alan, or any of the high-achieving professionals that are battling with Imposter Syndrome, this seems like a valid question, and one I was asked at a networking event two years ago, interestingly, by an HR director from a large global firm. "I'm so sick of everyone claiming they have Imposter Syndrome," she said. "Most of them are Oxbridge graduates with high-paying, secure jobs that net them 6-figures a year. And now even Michelle Obama! Oh poor me," she says, as she attempted to mimic Michelle Obama's voice, "I'm the First Lady, the world worships me, but still sometimes I feel like a fraud!"

Evidently, the woman in question had had her fill of high achievers claiming to suffer from Imposter Syndrome, but she had clearly not considered what lay beneath the surface of those achievements, and what those achievements cost.

It's a threat to your wellbeing

Underneath the successes and high achievements, Imposter Syndrome can create a real threat to your wellbeing. The fear of exposure, the discomfort with achievement and the resulting anxiety and stress – these not only interfere with your ability to accept and enjoy those achievements, they also have a negative impact on your mental health. The list of symptoms that have been catalogued in the research include: uncontrollable anxiety, burnout, emotional exhaustion, loss of motivation, underachievement, guilt and shame about success. All of these can leave you feeling even more inadequate and can also lead to depression.[6] For my clients, the risk of burnout from overworking, perfectionism and constant anxiety is a very real concern. Some have experienced burnout themselves in the past, while others have witnessed this in a colleague and so are aware of the risk for themselves.

It keeps you playing small

Beneath all the high achievements there's a heavy professional cost too: when you suffer from Imposter Syndrome you play small – for example, by keeping your head down to avoid being visible – something I found myself doing all through school and long after I started my career as a lawyer. How many times did I sit in a classroom or meeting room knowing I had something to contribute to the discussion, too paralysed by the fear of getting it wrong or saying something stupid to ever put my hand up or speak? Another feature of playing small is turning down opportunities either to avoid being found out and/ or because you are convinced that someone else is better qualified for the job. If your Imposter Syndrome is particularly acute, you may leave your job altogether and seek a role for which you are massively overqualified, as your way of trying to escape the fear of not being good enough.

It negatively affects your performance

If you have Imposter Syndrome, you're less efficient, effective and productive than you could be because you spend so much time second-guessing yourself and overworking in an attempt to make things perfect. Writing emails is a prime example of this, and one I know only too well. Writing emails, however short or trivial, triggers a compulsive need to check, reword and rephrase – requiring an amount of time and effort that is totally disproportionate to the importance of the message. This inefficiency also shows up in relation to tasks where there is a tendency to first procrastinate (because you're desperate to avoid what feels like an inevitable clash between the task and your abilities) and then exhaust yourself in a frenzy of fear-driven overactivity.

It hinders your ability to communicate

Because the fear of exposure in Imposter Syndrome sufferers is so real, even the most straight-forward communication feels like a risk that needs to be carefully managed. This leads you to habitually qualify everything you say with words like "perhaps" or "maybe" or "might", rather than stating your views confidently and convincingly. The result is that you are less effective at communicating because those around you feel the uncertainty and insecurity behind your words.

There is also the matter of background noise, which is common amongst my coaching clients and which I have experienced frequently myself. I'm referring to the internal background noise you have to contend with when you're trying to communicate. If you suffer from Imposter Syndrome, the strain of this will be all too familiar. At any given moment, your brain is not only trying to calculate what to say and how to say it, but also dealing with your internal voice telling you – at the same time as you are speaking – that what you are saying is wrong or stupid and/or how you are saying it is inarticulate and unclear. With so much going on internally, communicating clearly, concisely and confidently can feel like a Herculean challenge.

It's a shadowy presence

The intensity of the Imposter Syndrome experience can vary. At times, it is ongoing – a constant feeling of low-level anxiety that makes every communication or action more stressful and exhausting than it needs to be. At other times, your Imposter Syndrome can present as a full-blown crisis. This typically happens in response to a specific event or circumstance that acts as a trigger – when you receive negative feedback, for example, or when the risk of exposure is particularly high, such as when you are about to deliver a presentation to a client or you are asked to take the lead on a project. Thanks to its shifting nature, Imposter Syndrome can feel like a shadowy presence in the background, that never quite goes away and that lies in wait for the next opportunity to hold you back.

Once you consider the threat that Imposter Syndrome can pose to your wellbeing and your work – through its effect on your performance, your willingness to seize opportunities and your communication skills – then, suddenly, all those successes and achievements don't seem quite so joyous. The reality is that beneath the surface of those successes, you are fighting a constant battle against self-doubt that not only prevents you from enjoying it but makes that success hard to bear.

The internal battle against this unique form of self-doubt is challenging enough for anyone.

But when you're a person of colour trying to succeed in a white world, it doesn't end there. Your Imposter Syndrome isn't just an internal battle, it's also an external one: a battle against systemic bias. We're going to learn more about this in the next chapter.

Summary

»   Imposter Syndrome is no ordinary form of self-doubt. The more you achieve, the worse it gets.

»   Research shows that as many as 75% of the population have suffered from Imposter Syndrome at some point in their lives.

»   Imposter Syndrome has no limits: it spans gender, religion, industry and sexual orientation. It occurs where there is real or perceived difference from the apparent norm.

»   Imposter Syndrome is prevalent in high achievers, although you wouldn't know this as it's so well hidden.

»   Imposter Syndrome is an internal battle against self-doubt that affects your wellbeing and your work and is a barrier to achieving your potential.

YOU ARE AN IMPOSTER

"It doesn't go away, that feeling of 'I don't know if the world will take me seriously'."

– MICHELLE OBAMA

I n the previous chapter, we discussed what Imposter Syndrome is, its origins and who it affects. We discussed why Imposter Syndrome is a unique form of self-doubt and the impact it has on your wellbeing and performance at work.

In this chapter, I will show you why Imposter Syndrome is different for high potential people of colour like us who are striving to succeed in a white world. We'll take a closer look at the systemic bias you encounter in the workplace and how this makes your Imposter Syndrome both unique and more acute, and at the experiences you are subjected to in the workplace that contribute to that. I'll be sharing examples from my own personal experience, as well as the experiences of high potential people of colour I have coached or who have attended one of my Imposter Syndrome events.

This chapter will help you understand why your Imposter Syndrome is different to that experienced by your white peers. But you'll also discover that you're not alone. I've been there. Many other high potential people of colour like you have been and still are where you are. We all know what it's like to try to progress within a system that is riddled with bias. As a result of reading this chapter, you'll understand why the solutions to Imposter Syndrome that work for your white colleagues and friends aren't enough for you. You'll realise that while they are fighting a single battle, you are fighting two. You need a solution to Imposter Syndrome that will help you overcome both, and you'll find that solution in this book.

By now you will have a clear understanding of Imposter Syndrome and you may have recalled moments in your life where you've experienced it. Perhaps it's something you're struggling with in your life right now and you can feel how it is negatively affecting your self-esteem, your mental health, or your performance at work. You may feel, in the words of one of my clients, that it's time to "stop sabotaging myself and give myself permission to have a better future". You've also seen how common Imposter Syndrome is, particularly amongst high achievers. So common, in fact, that it begs the question: if Imposter

"

Your success and achievements to date have propelled you into a white world that, at a systemic level, was neither built nor designed for you to thrive.

"

Syndrome is so widespread – crossing cultures, genders and industries – what is so special about Imposter Syndrome in people of colour? Why is this book about me?

Your Imposter Syndrome is a war on two fronts

Your Imposter Syndrome is an altogether more complex and literal experience than that of your white peers and colleagues. You are not just fighting an internal battle – the battle against self-doubt. You are also fighting an external battle – the battle against systemic bias. I've been empowering others to own their Imposter Syndrome through my keynote talks and my coaching programmes for over six years and I've been battling it my whole life. I've surveyed thousands of high achievers in some of the world's most prestigious and competitive firms and organisations about their experiences of Imposter Syndrome. What I have learned is that when it comes to progressing your career, your race and ethnicity are major aggravating factors that intensify your experience of Imposter Syndrome at an identity level, and take the task of fulfilling your potential in a white world to a whole new and immensely challenging level.

Let's face it. Your success and achievements to date have propelled you into a white world that, at a systemic level, was neither built nor designed for you to thrive. There is no well-trodden path for you to follow and few, if any, leaders or role models to inspire you and show you how it's done. You are typically the only person of colour in the room and you are more likely than not to have been subjected to implicit or explicit forms of racism. The way your whole working environment is built repeatedly reinforces the message: "You are an imposter. You shouldn't be here". For you, Imposter Syndrome is not just an internal crisis. It's an external reality.

The culture of your organisation doesn't have to use the word "fraud" for you to feel like an imposter. It doesn't need to tell you explicitly that you don't deserve your success for you to question whether you belong there, and it doesn't need to threaten you with exposure in order for you to feel that your career is hanging permanently in the balance. These messages float through the corridors of the all-white partnership, they echo through the air in the all-white meetings and reverberate through the public school accents and the in-jokes that you don't understand. The message coming from all around you is: "You're a fraud. You don't deserve your success. Any minute now you'll be exposed." Thanks to the lack of diversity, inclusion and equality in your environment, Imposter Syndrome hits you in a whole different way and at a much deeper level. You feel like an imposter. Because you really are one.

These are the experiences of high potential people of colour like you who I have either coached, worked with or encountered in the white corporate world. How many of these scenarios can you relate to?

"I didn't really see anyone who looks like me doing what I did, and this whole imposter thing, it's a real thing. Especially when I've come from rooms that are filled with just white people and me."

– CANDICE CARTY-WILLIAMS

"There's no one like me"

When you're a person of colour, there is no obvious path leading you to achieve success in a white world. Unlike the majority of your white peers, doing well at school, attending Oxbridge, or a Russell Group University was never a given. In some cases I have come across (and as you'll see in Chapter 3, my own story), it was highly unlikely. Many high potential people of colour who are working in a white corporate world are the first generation in their family to attend university. Perhaps you are one of them? This is in stark contrast to the experience of your average white person who works at an investment bank or law firm in the City of London. As a result, people of colour feel there's no one like them at work – no one who has had the same experiences growing up, the same struggles and hurdles to overcome in order to get where they are.

"It's easy for some"

I remember delivering a talk on Imposter Syndrome at one of the top US law firms in 2014. I will never forget the moment when a well-spoken white gentleman in the back of the audience shared his story of how he came to be working at one of the world's most recognised law firms. It was a short story: "I did law at university because that's what all my friends were doing. And when it came to getting a training contract, to be honest, I didn't really give it much thought. I just applied, and I got in." Though I was careful not to show it at the time, I was startled by the stark contrast between how casually and accidentally this man had landed one of the most lucrative and prestigious of careers and my own journey to an equivalent role at a similar firm. I'll share my very different journey with you in Chapter 3.

LISA'S STORY

The feeling of having taken an unconventional or wrong route to where she is, has always been a challenge for Lisa, who I met at a networking event recently. Lisa went to her local school in Croydon, London, and gained her law degree from Southampton University, the first in her

family to attend university. Despite winning a training contract at a top tier law firm, she can't shake the insecurity of
not having attended private school or read law at Oxford or
Cambridge, as it seemed so many of her white colleagues
had. For Lisa, it was irrelevant that not all of her peers
attended Oxbridge. As one of only four people of colour in
her intake of over 50 graduate recruits, she feels like someone who, in her words, "slipped through the net".

Does this sound familiar? Were you the first generation in
your family to attend university? Were you the first to be
born outside your country of origin, or to have a white-col-
lar job with potential?

It's harder to connect with others when your background
and life experience is so different. You've taken the road
less travelled to get here, which makes your success arriving at this point all the more remarkable. But the experience provides yet more validation for your Imposter Syndrome because it sends the message there's something
fraudulent or wrong in you being here.

"I'm the only one in the room"

If you're fortunate enough to have joined your organisation as a junior and you're one of several people of colour

at your level, the feeling that you are on an equal footing with your white peers doesn't last for long. Within a few years, the ethnic diversity which many organisations boast at graduate recruitment level drops alarmingly as more and more people of colour leave. If you are one of the few who choose to stay, this can cause you to question not only your decision to stay on, but also the legitimacy of any ambition you have to progress to the top and your likelihood of being able to do so.

JON'S STORY

This was Jon's experience. When he joined his firm as a management consultant in the City of London, almost half of his intake was of mixed ethnicity. Jon felt he was part of the new generation of black professionals who were taking the City by storm and who would, in years to come, transform the complexion of leadership. But Jon's optimism for being part of the first wave of diverse leadership was soon stifled. One by one his black, Indian and Asian friends began to leave. By the time he was starting his fourth year at the firm, he was the only person of colour from his intake remaining.

ASHANTI'S STORY

These are the thoughts that haunt Ashanti, one of only two black associates in her whole firm of 140 lawyers. When she joined as part of a graduate scheme, she was one of six people of colour, which amounted to over ten percent of her graduate intake. Now she is three years qualified and wondering if she has made a mistake. The higher up the ranks she gets, the lonelier and more isolated she feels. There are no partners of colour in her firm, and there never have been. There are no role models of colour in her firm, so there is no one to look up to and no one who inspires her to stay. Ashanti likes her boss and enjoys the work. But whether it's at client meetings or after-work drinks; departmental off-sites or client pitches, she is always, always the only person of colour in the room, and it's starting to bother her.

Can you relate to these experiences? Did you join your organisation as part of a diverse cohort, only to discover, when you took stock a few years later, that everyone had gone? Look around you right now. Are you the only one left?

When you're the only one left in the room you start to ask yourself questions. Did I make the right decision to stay? Did everyone else get it right? The experience of being the only one in the room provides yet more validation for your Imposter Syndrome because it reinforces the message that you shouldn't be there at all.

"I don't fit in"

The differences which make you feel you have little in common with your white peers go beyond your ability to bond while sharing childhood memories over a drink after work. These differences are made evident by the cultural norms and practices that are built into the infrastructure of predominantly white organisations. These range from the dos and don'ts of what to wear to building client loyalty through extravagant corporate entertaining. As a result, both your access to clients and ability to attract the right opportunities can be compromised, simply because you weren't exposed to these rules and experiences growing up.

AN OUTSIDER LOOKING IN

I remember many instances of feeling that I didn't fit in as a lawyer at Allen & Overy. Client events frequently involved activities I had never done or in some cases even heard of before, like clay pigeon shooting, for example (you'll hear my story about this in Chapter 3). As a person of colour growing up on a council estate in Birmingham, you could go your whole life and never even hear of a concept like clay pigeon shooting. But it wasn't just eclectic (to me, at least) events like this. Even tennis, and the idea of going to Wimbledon – a standard form of corporate entertainment – was so far removed from my experience and yet another scenario in which I felt I didn't fit. I will never forget my first visit to Wimbledon with a senior associate to entertain a client. It was great to be out of the office for the day. But I was an outsider looking in. Unlike my white peers, I had never even held a tennis racket until the age of 17 – and that was only briefly when I attended (as a spectator, obviously) a local village tennis competition with some of my white tennis-playing friends.

Have you ever felt that everyone else has had an experience that you haven't? Maybe for you it was a golf day with clients or eating at high-end restaurants where all your white peers seem to know exactly what to do. Do you find yourself worrying about things your white peers don't have to worry about? What to wear to a particular event, for example, or understanding the lingo others use?

As human beings, we are genetically programmed to want to fit in. In the early days of our evolution, our survival depended on it. Now, although we no longer face the dangers and hazards our ancestors did, our need to fit in remains. That's why not fitting in is so painful. Every time you experience being apart from the crowd – because you don't share their knowledge or experience – you experience it as a threat. It compounds the feeling that you don't belong and increases the fear that you'll be exposed.

"I have no role models"

Most senior positions in firms and organisations are white, which means that if you're a high potential person of colour looking for role models to inspire you or show you how it's done, you will struggle to find one. Role models are important. They inspire you and motivate you because they are evidence of what is possible. Role models encourage you to be more than you think you can be or your circumstances tell you that you can be – which is why role models of colour are so important, and the absence of them has such a significant effect.

77

THERE'S NO ONE HERE I WANT TO BE

I don't recall there being any black lawyers ahead of me when I was an associate at Allen & Overy, and there were certainly no black partners. There were some senior associates of colour, but out of the hundreds of lawyers in the firm at that time, these were an anomaly. In the London office, at the time, I remember being aware of only 2 or 3 out of over 900 lawyers. Of course, there were plenty of people of colour in the firm, but these were either bringing the post or standing by the front door as security. You didn't see people of colour heading off to meetings, briefcase in hand or sitting behind desks in their own offices. This all had a significant impact on me when, as a mid-level associate, I was ready to make a decision about my next move. I had always wanted to be a partner and it was only logical that I stay at Allen & Overy and make a go of it. But I remember looking at the all-white, mostly male partnership, and consciously thinking, "I can't relate to you. Or you. Or you. I don't fit. There's no one here I want to be."

Is this your experience? When you look up and ahead of you, what do you see? Is there a leader of colour who inspires you? Are there senior people of colour who are paving the way and serving as proof that it can be done?

Looking at the data I'm fairly confident your answer is no. The 2017 Parker Review of ethnic diversity in business revealed that over 50% of FTSE 100 companies had no ethnic representation on their boards whatsoever. Today, despite the push to increase diversity on boards, those numbers show little sign of improvement. According to the new Parker Review report published this year[7], 37% of FTSE 100 companies surveyed still do not have any ethnic minority representation on their boards. With so few role models to look up to, the message you receive is that you're an imposter: you're in the wrong place; people like you don't make it to the top and why should it be any different for you?

"I can't be myself"

When the dominant culture is white, what is valued and rewarded tends to reflect that culture. The result is that people of colour find that behavioural norms they've inherited from their culture are often at odds with those that are considered valuable at work. It's common for a person of colour to receive feedback on a personality trait or a particular behaviour that they need to change or improve if they want to succeed.

_____

MINESH'S STORY

Minesh is an accountant of Indian heritage who has been at the same global accounting firms for 20 years. At his first attempt at partnership eight years ago, Minesh was told he didn't cut it. He needed to adapt his communication style to convey more authority and gravitas, and bring more aggression and forcefulness when representing his clients. The news that he would not be promoted to partner after years of dedication to his clients and the firm was devastating. But what hurt the most was the suggestion that if he wanted to get the promotion, he'd effectively have to be someone he was not.

Minesh grew up in a culture where respect and deference were valued more highly than aggression and forcefulness. For him, being asked to leave behind everything he'd been taught in order to achieve the promotion he believed he'd earned was a moral compromise he did not want to have to make. What should he do? Be his authentic self and give up his dream of promotion or compromise his authenticity in order to fulfil his goals?

_____

Does this sound familiar to you? Do you look at the behaviour of those around you who are singled out for praise or promotion and feel a huge disconnect? Perhaps you have an accent, or preferred style of dressing, that you feel you have to tone down or cover-up in order to be valued? Or maybe you've been told to?

Research shows that when we're more authentic at work we contribute more and perform better. We're also happier and more fulfilled. Striking the balance between your authentic self and the expectations of your organisational environment is a challenge for any employee. But for you, the pervasiveness of a dominant white culture makes this harder.

Suggestions that you change your style or behaviour, however well they are presented as feedback to help you improve, often send the message: "We'll value you more if you're less like you and more like us". It is hard not to read this as a message: You don't belong here. You're an imposter.

"I'm treated differently"

When you're a person of colour it can feel like you draw a level of attention and scrutiny that your white peers don't. When you receive negative feedback on behaviour that you see your white colleagues exhibiting all the time, it reeks of double standards. I've heard stories of people of colour being told to soften their communication style in organisations where leaders at the top are revered and renowned for their combative style. People of colour are criticised as stubborn or intransigent, while their white colleague displaying the same behaviour is praised for being tenacious.

JESSICA'S STORY

Jessica, who works in asset management, gets this a lot. As the only black woman in her team and the most senior black woman in her organisation, she feels she is constantly subjected to these double standards. Frequent references to her being "scary" and someone you "don't want to cross", and to her having an aggressive leadership style, are hugely frustrating. She sees her peers and other leaders adopting a similar style to her own without being subject to scrutiny or criticism. For her, the message is brutally clear: it's OK for us to do it, but not you. You're too much. You need to tone it down.

Can you relate to this? Have you ever come out of a review or received feedback on your way of working which seemed at odds with what is praised in others around you? Or perhaps it's less blatant. Maybe you see white peers being promoted for qualities you feel you are being discouraged to display.

The feeling that you are being treated differently and that there are a different set of rules (or standards) for your white peers is enormously debilitating. When the message is "we can do it but you can't" or "be less like you and more like us", it tells you very clearly: you're an imposter.

"I'm disrespected"

Alarmingly and disappointingly, people of colour are still being subjected to racism in its various guises at work. While this may be less explicit than in years gone by, it remains. Stories abound of white colleagues (often those in more senior positions) making derogatory comments about racial ancestry or sharing careless and often hurtful jokes that promote racial stereotypes. Sometimes the racism is more discreet and lurks behind behaviour that seems innocuous, but sends a very negative message.

ADEBAYO'S STORY

I met Adebayo at a networking event last year. When I repeated his name back to him to ensure that I'd heard it correctly, it felt like I'd inadvertently erected a wall between us. I'd clearly done something to offend him and felt compelled to find out. Adebayo told me about his frustration with no one getting his name right at work. "Four years, and they still don't know how to say it. I'm sick of it. And when I make a point of correcting them when they get it wrong, they act like I'm being unnecessarily precious and serious about it. There's no respect. No respect at all."

I've heard so many different versions of Adebayo's story all over the City. Sometimes it's about names. Other times it manifests as an exaggerated enthusiasm for trying to understand what it's like "where you're from".

Does this mirror your experience? Are you being subjected to micro-aggressions like "can I touch your hair" and "all black people are good dancers"? Perhaps the comments you've been subjected to are more offensive and direct – references to you always eating curry if you're of Indian or Pakistani descent for example.

Nothing sends a clearer message that you shouldn't be here than an overtly racist remark from a white senior leader or the stream of micro-aggressions being inflicted by your white peers. The message you receive is unequivocal: we don't understand you. You don't fit in. You're an imposter.

"I'm undervalued"

Being continuously reminded that your experience and culture are different from what is perceived as the norm can leave you feeling undervalued. What about the quality of your work? How about the commitment you've shown to the job or the sacrifices you've made (late nights in the office; working weekends; putting work ahead of your personal relationships and sometimes even your physical health)? When these go unacknowledged, or they are superseded by feedback that focuses on your appearance or communication style, you feel you're being taken for granted and that no matter what you do, you'll never be good enough.

RICHARD'S STORY

Another classic racial stereotype that alienates people of colour is of the angry black male. Richard is over six-feet-tall and has a gentle, easy manner. One of five boys, and the son of a proud Caribbean mother, he is well-reared in the art of speaking up and communicating his message in order to be heard. But what is considered an admirable quality in his community is considered something of a liability in his workplace. Richard has lost count of the number of times he's been told to tone it down because he's coming across as too strident. "I'm a 6ft-tall black man who stands up straight and knows how to hold my own in a conversation," he told me. "I could be reciting a nursery rhyme and these guys would still find me threatening. This whole idea that I'm some kind of angry black man with an axe to grind is not only insulting, it's way off the mark."

Have you ever had that feeling that your white peers and leaders don't see your work, they only see you? And the "you" that they see is someone whose behaviour isn't quite right or who, as a whole, is not the right fit? Or perhaps it's about your relationships with others in the office. Has "No one knows you" been used as the reason why you're not being put forward for promotion this year?

For Richard, what should have been a quality that could work as an asset to the firm (who wouldn't want a six-feet tall, confident, outspoken lawyer on their side?), has been undermined and undervalued.

The cost of Imposter Syndrome for people of colour

Imposter Syndrome has the same negative impact on high potential people of colour as it does on any other demographic group. You play small, let opportunities pass you by and the fear of exposure drives you to perfectionism. The stress and anxiety your Imposter Syndrome produces can have a negative effect on your mental health and be detrimental to your wellbeing.

You step down

But there's more. When you're a high potential person of colour there's a whole other challenge. It's not only "how do I overcome feeling like an imposter?" it's "how do I overcome being treated like one?" The systemic bias at work makes you feel like this is a battle you cannot win and so you either leave or you resign yourself to a career path where the financial rewards are lower and the opportunities for fulfilling your true potential are fewer.

The data proves this. Rare Recruitment's research into BAME (Black, Asian and Minority Ethnic – as this group is defined in the report) attrition in the top law firms in the City of London has shown that a BAME lawyer's tenure is 18 months shorter than that of their white counterparts. This amounts to you spending 20% less time in your jobs. Rare's research into the individual experiences of those they surveyed shows that the lack of diversity, the overt and covert incidents of racism, the inability to be authentic and the non-inclusive culture are directly responsible for this.

The personal cost

While this failure to retain diverse talent is, of course, bad news for organisations, there is also a personal cost to you. When you walk away or step aside from the career opportunities, you stifle your own potential and miss out on the opportunity to evolve into the next version of yourself. This is the version of yourself that is more confident and experienced and which, as a result of the obstacles you have had to overcome to get where you are, is more resilient, powerful and valuable than ever before.

The aspirational cost to others

There is also the aspirational cost to the next generation of leaders of colour and the communities of colour around you. They are seeing their highest achievers finally gain access to the positions of influence and financial reward previously reserved exclusively for their white peers, only to see them walk away from those opportunities – sending the message that it can't be done. Without you, there will be fewer people of colour in the places where all the money is held, influence is wielded and the biggest decisions are made. This means fewer role models of colour to inspire those behind you, and fewer of us to battle systemic bias from within.

Now for the good news

If all of this is making you feel a little despondent, I have news for you. The uniqueness of your experience as a person of colour in a white world is that if you want to succeed, your difference is your greatest opportunity. Most people think that the solution to Imposter Syndrome is to convince yourself that you're just like everyone else – as good as they are, as entitled to their place as they are, as well-positioned to succeed. But blending in and being like everyone else isn't why you're here. You are an imposter. You were born to stand out.

The colour of your skin makes you stand out from the rest, which means others have no choice but to notice you. But this is just the beginning. As soon as you allow for how unique you are because of how different you look, or the difference in your culture, you open the door to allowing in all the other things that are special and unique about you. There are things that separate you not only from your all-white peers and colleagues and friends, but from other people of colour too: your life experiences, your failures and achievements, your ambitions and aspirations. These unique aspects are the key to your value and the source of your power, and they are the secret to winning the battle against self-doubt. We're going to explore all of this in Part III. But first, we have a different battle to fight: the battle against systemic bias.

Summary

»   As a high potential person of colour you suffer a unique form of Imposter Syndrome: you don't just feel like an imposter. You are one.

»   You are an imposter because you are striving to succeed in a system which is biased against you.

»   You are undervalued, disrespected and excluded.

»   You are treated differently and can't be yourself at work.

»   You have no role models and you're typically the only person of colour in the room.

»   In order to succeed, you must fight a war on two fronts: the internal battle against self-doubt and the external battle against systemic bias.

»   When you don't succeed, not only is there a cost to your organisation, there's a personal cost to you and an aspirational cost to your community.

»   You are an imposter. You were born to stand out.

FINDING YOUR POWER

"Success is to be measured not so much by the position that one has reached in life as by the obstacles which he has overcome while trying to succeed."

- BOOKER T. WASHINGTON

In the previous chapter, we looked at how your experience of Imposter Syndrome as a person of colour is unique. While others are fighting an internal battle against self-doubt, you are also fighting a battle against systemic bias.

In this chapter, I'm going to share some of my experiences as a person of colour who has been battling this form of Imposter Syndrome my whole life, and who has learned how to win. Like you, I am an imposter. I have felt undervalued and disrespected. I've been excluded and there have been times when I felt I couldn't be myself at work. I've had no black role models and I have almost always been the only person of colour in the room. But that didn't stop me. Being treated like an imposter didn't hold me back. I found that even during the darkest experiences of my life and the most challenging moments of my career I was able to find my power and that's how I've been able to succeed.

This chapter will remind you that although you are a member of a minority group, you have more power than you think. Being a person of colour trying to succeed in a white world may feel like a lonely endeavour. You think you're the only one in the room (because you literally are, or because you are one of a tiny minority), but you're so much more than that. You're the first. You are the front-runner, the ground-breaker, the trailblazer. You are exceptional, outstanding, extraordinary. The reason you haven't felt this before now is because you've forgotten your power. You've been waiting for the system to be fixed and for things outside and around you to change. When you do that, you give away all your power and overlook your ability to change things on the inside. It's time to reclaim that power and use it.

"Statistics can't trap me"

Let me start from the beginning.

According to the UK children's charity Barnardo's, children with an offending parent are twice as likely to drop out of school, extremely likely to suffer mental health problems and three times as likely to become offenders themselves[8].

My family contributed their fair share to those statistics. Interactions between members of my family and the police were a regular feature of my childhood. Someone was always being arrested or questioned by the police. It wasn't uncommon to hear a knock on the door that told you instantly that there was a man or woman in uniform on the other side with a list of questions that no one knew how to answer. One of the strongest memories for me, as the youngest sister at the time, was the feeling of relief when my brothers walked through the door at the end of the day. It meant they hadn't been arrested (or if they'd been arrested, they hadn't been charged). This was the 1970s and 1980s in the poorest parts of Birmingham and London, when strangers came up to you in the street and called you "nigger" to your face and told you to go back to where you came from. It was long before Black Lives Matter and the injustices of racial inequality, made prominent by the killing of George Floyd, captured the collective consciousness. You may be old enough to have experienced this time yourself.

My early childhood was a time and place where if you were a young black girl you had your first child before your 16th birthday and gave birth to their brothers and sisters, often with different fathers, in quick succession. If you were lucky enough to stay out of trouble and could afford to feed your children, you got to keep them. If you weren't and you couldn't, they'd be taken away. Meanwhile, if you were a typical black boy where I grew up, it was normal to play truant from school and get caught up in a life of petty crime that not only alleviated your boredom and frustration, but also provided a short-lived respite from the harsh reality of having no money, no positive role models and limited prospects. Stealing car radios was not always done for fun. Often, it was because it was the easiest thing to trade in for money to buy food. It was a world where a young, single black mother who struggled to feed her two young children would swipe food from the shelves of the local supermarket using her 4- and 5-year-old children as cover. Crime of all shapes and varieties was commonplace. Sometimes you got away with it. Sometimes you didn't. None of this was hypothetical. This was the reality of how I, my siblings and the people of colour in my community existed, and it was hard.

At the age of six, I was sent off to boarding school and the seeds of my Imposter Syndrome were sown. I know you'd love to know how this happened; how a young black girl from a poor black family ended up in a wealthy white world, and so would I. What I can tell you is that one day I was home and the next day I wasn't. One minute I was sneaking downstairs with my brother in the middle of the night, making sugar and white bread sandwiches, and the next minute I was lying in a dormitory with 15 white girls being told to settle down by the matron standing sentry at the door. One minute I was surrounded by people who looked like me, the next I was the only person of colour in the room. And I've been the only one in the room, or one of a tiny minority of people of colour in the room, ever since. Always in the minority. Always the imposter.

It was a beautiful school and I thrived. I was the only black kid in the school and I excelled. I was a compulsive over-achiever, driven by my Imposter Syndrome to win all the prizes in all the subjects year after year after year. I dominated the leadership boards and I set sporting record after sporting record. By the time I left that school I'd been Head of House and Head Girl, and three other black kids had joined the school. I wasn't the only one in the school. I was the first.

It could have been different. I could have rebelled and reacted and refused. I could have let that lack of diversity and isolation be the reason I couldn't succeed. But instead, I fought. I seized every opportunity and I went all in. This took me all the way to the top. Even though it was hard, and even though there were no guarantees. Statistics couldn't trap me, and they shouldn't trap you either.

"Names won't stop me"

LADY OF THE JUNGLE

The memories I have of my primary school music lessons remain vivid to this day. Rows of wooden desks, sunlight streaming through old draughty windows and a music teacher who was larger than life. He had big bi-focal glasses that teetered perilously on the edge of his nose, wiry strands of white hair peeking out of his nostrils and a globule of spit that clung obstinately to his upper lip. My music teacher was difficult to relate to, but he was not an unkind man. He was clumsy and mumbly, but passionate about his subject, and worked hard to engage a lively spirited class, asking question after question, calling all of us by name to solicit an answer. Except that the name he used to call on me wasn't like anybody else's name. It wasn't really a name at all.

"Tom! Settle down at the back!"

"Nicola, look this way!"

"Well done, Jane, excellent work!"

And to me: "Lady of the Jungle at the back! What's the answer?"

The first time it happened it cut through me like a knife. Straight through the chest, causing my breath to catch in my throat, my whole body to flood with shame. The snickering erupted around me. There was laughter and the mocking sound of jungle noises that the boys in the back row did nothing to conceal.

Lady of the Jungle. A name rolls carelessly off someone's tongue, and then it sticks.

I am fiercely protective and proud of my collection of books. They are, quite literally, a paper trail of my life to date, which makes some of them pretty old! On the desk next to me as I write this chapter, sits an old thesaurus I turn to time and again when I'm writing. It is pure coincidence that two days ago, when I began work on editing this chapter, I opened up my thesaurus to the first page and couldn't believe what I saw:

"The Viney Music Prize awarded to Caroline Heath. 1986."

Again, things could have been different. I could have let racism block me but I didn't. I found my power and I stayed on track and I won the battle. Even though it was hard. Even though I might have failed. Names won't stop me, and they shouldn't stop you either.

"Stereotypes won't limit me"

It wasn't all bad. I built some incredible friendships during those early school years that to this day I still remember with fondness. But those friendships had their own role to play as part of a system that aggravated my Imposter Syndrome by treating me like an imposter.

I remember walking down a path with a group of girlfriends laughing and giggling and doing what schoolgirls do. I was always slightly wary at these times. The conversations would often start off innocently, but then quickly veer off into what for me was dangerous and unfamiliar territory – dangerous because one false statement, and I'd expose just how much of an imposter I really was. Like the time I said I'd never heard of Premium Bonds and what were they and everyone thought I was joking. And the time, at the age of 13, I admitted I'd never seen the sea. And the conversations about hair and dentist appointments and mums taking daughters shopping for bras left me scrambling for invented family stories and little white lies that would throw them off the scent of my difference, and hide my Imposter Syndrome. But I stuck with it because I knew, surely, it was only a matter of time before I gained what every schoolgirl has ever wanted since the dawn of school, and that is to be accepted. And when it came it was not what I had expected. It was the opposite of what I'd wanted:

"Caroline, y'know. You're not like real black people at all, you're actually really nice."

I could have been crushed by those words and the many other versions that have come to me over the years. I could have given up the fight and let the racism hold me down. I could have resented their exclusion and tied myself in knots over not being able to be myself. But, instead, I kept fighting those battles. I stayed on track and I stepped into my power as someone whose gift it was to challenge racial stereotypes and change people's minds. Racial stereotyping didn't hold me back. It shouldn't hold you back either.

"Being powerless doesn't work for me"

PLACES LIKE THAT

I was sitting at the table in the kitchen of someone's house. We moved around a lot when I was young – often suddenly and without warning – so I don't remember where we were, and I don't remember who else was there.

I remember only that my mum was holding an envelope and that the contents of that envelope would decide my fate.

I watched in terrified silence as my mother tore open the envelope and pulled a letter out. I couldn't read the words, but I could see through the thick white sheet of paper that the message was brief. My mother's face as she read its contents said it all. I was shocked and devastated. Hadn't I done everything right? I was the top student. I'd won everything, exceeded everybody and blown the roof off the ceiling of other people's expectations. "They'd be lucky to have me," my maths teacher had told me.

"I'm sorry, my darling, you didn't get in," my mother said, with poorly disguised bitterness and anger. "It's not your fault. It's because places like that don't want people like us."

Places like that. Places like grammar schools in Kent with bright green sports fields and that are full of white people who have perfect families, who have cars that work, parents who come to parents' evenings, and where the students have tennis lessons and ski holidays and live in houses they own. This was the mid-1980s. Poor inner-city black people did not go to all-white middle-class schools in the countryside.

"Places like that don't want people like us." In that compassionate gesture, the universe offered me a way out. A get out of jail free card. A reason and an excuse for not achieving or getting the result I so desperately wanted. This wasn't my fault. It wasn't about me or my ability. This was about a system we couldn't change, inequality we couldn't fix and injustice we couldn't right.

There it was, from my mother's mouth. The "no matter what you do you'll never be good enough". I was 13 and I was being told that there's a system beyond my control that will kill my dreams and hold me back, and there's nothing I can do about it.

And with a steely calm, I knew that that would never be enough for me. That reasoning, however justified or however often we saw evidence of it, was one that I could not accept.

Look back on the key milestones in your life and you'll realise that the moments that change you aren't the moments in which the drama happens. They are the moments immediately afterwards. It wasn't the letter. It wasn't what my mother said that counted. It's how I reacted to it. It was to be one of the most pivotal moments of my life.

Places like that. People like us. You are powerless. Think that if you want, but I can't and I won't. Because if I accept that the obstacle is the colour of my skin then I'm powerless because it's the one thing that will never change. I didn't want the truth. I wanted something I could work with. My mother didn't know it at the time, but the explanation that she offered me for my rejection from Cranbrook Grammar School was a critical moment. My decision to reject that rejection changed my life.

When I joined Cranbrook Grammar School as a boarder in 1986 – the very same school which had sent me the rejection letter less than a year earlier – I was once again the only black pupil in the school. Again, you'll be looking for answers: if they turned her down, how did she end up going there? And I don't have all the answers to that question either, except that a determined mother and a stubborn daughter are not as powerless as they may seem. Maybe you can guess what happened next. By the time I left Cranbrook in 1990, I was joint head of school, I had a bookshelf full of prizes and other people of colour had joined the school. To top it all, I was on my way to Cambridge.

Places like that.

It could have been different. The day of the rejection letter, I had every justification in the world to give up because the system was against me and everything out-side of me needed to change. But I wasn't willing to wait to be included. I wasn't prepared to wait for someone else to fix it. Powerlessness against an unequal system doesn't work for me. It shouldn't work for you.

"Setbacks won't stop me"

While my teenage friends were listening to Bryan Adams, Phil Collins and enjoying all the best that 80s pop music had to offer, the soundtrack to my teenage years was a little more raw and real.

CAMBRIDGE INTERVIEW

I can't remember the date when my mother left and the letters started. But I do remember how the letterbox would creak in protest every time the postman pushed one of those crisp white envelopes through the door, and how that envelope would float its way down to the floor and land with a tap on the tattered mat.

Creak. Pause. Tap. Creak. Pause. Tap. Day after day after day.

Even while I was sheltered away at Cranbrook, I knew those letters were landing on our doormat every day, terrorising my brother with their capitalised warnings and terrifying threats:

EVICTION NOTICE FOR NON-PAYMENT OF RENT.
COURT PROCEEDINGS PENDING.

Ask 10 different people what the perfect conditions for taking GCSEs and A-levels and getting a place at a university like Cambridge are, and you'll probably get 10 different answers. But what I'm sure they'll all agree on is that, in an ideal world, a 13-year-old girl and her 14-year-old brother shouldn't be left living alone and have to find their own way to pay gas and electricity bills and hustle to find the money for food. That in an ideal world that same girl wouldn't have to resort to building a desk out of four spare car tyres and a section of MDF which her brother had acquired from the local junkyard so she could study each day, only to have to dismantle and rebuild them into a makeshift bed to sleep on at night.

I'd like to think that my circumstances were unique or unusual and that you're finding nothing relatable in my story. But for many inner-city children of colour, situations like this are their reality. The conditions for everything, let alone studying, are far from perfect. They face social and economic challenges that many of their white peers could not even begin to imagine. Life knocks them down as children and they have to pick themselves up. They have to suck it all up and somehow find a way through.

In the days running up to my interview for Cambridge University, I was anxious. In all honestly, I was terrified and started cursing the day I agreed, at the insistence of my history teacher Mr Norton, to submit myself to this process and wondered how I would recover when I failed. It had taken over a decade to construct my wafer-thin veneer of confidence and I didn't know what I would do if it was shattered by the rejection.

The night before the big day, I found an old alarm clock in a kitchen draw and set it for an ungodly hour that would give me plenty of time to get to Cambridge for the stream of interviews that were lined up. I barely slept.

Except that I must have slept a little because when I woke up the next morning and looked at the clock, something wasn't right. After blinking several times in disbelief, my eyes fell with horror on the motionless hands. The battery was dead. The alarm hadn't gone off. I had overslept.

My brain was like lightning. There was no way in this universe I would make it from Camberwell to Cambridge in time for my interview. I'd landed the biggest opportunity I'd ever had in my life, bigger than most people have in a lifetime, and I'd blown it before it had even begun.

I cried. I sobbed my devastated, disappointed heart out. I felt a surge of anger at myself for not being the sort of kid with a mum at home to wake them up on time,

"

The conditions are never perfect. They are sometimes horrendous.

"

discuss what they were wearing over breakfast together, and then drive them up the motorway in a car rehearsing interview questions and telling them how great they are. I cried because my mum wasn't there, my dad was far away and no one around me seemed to understand what was at stake. I howled at how useless I was, how undeserving I felt and how stupid I'd been in thinking I could gain access to a place I had no right to be.

The memory of my mother's voice from years before came back to me: *Places like that. People like us...*

All of a sudden, my brain was like lightning. The sobbing stopped. And I got to work. When you've spent years faking your mother's voice on the phone and forging permission slips for school, you get really good at it. With nerves of steel, I found the number of Corpus Christi College (the college within the university I was applying to) and, in the most adult voice I could muster, asked to speak to the Director of Studies (one of two professors scheduled to interview me that day). In a voice that conveyed an authority and maturity I didn't feel, I told him that I was Caroline's mother, that we'd been caught in a minor collision on the M11 (but please don't worry, everyone is fine), and that my daughter Caroline, although shaken, was adamant that she would not miss her interviews today. Could they possibly postpone the interviews until the end of the day to give us time to arrive? "Oh, you'd both be willing to stay late to meet Caroline? Oh, how very kind and understanding of you. I can't thank you enough…"

––––––––––––––––––––––

It could have been different. Everything about that situation screamed "imposter" to me at the time, and I'll be honest with you – when I think of how close I came to not making it to Cambridge that day – it still does. I could have given up. I could have taken it as a sign. I could have used it as an excuse not to risk failure. But I fought that battle and I showed up, even though it was hard and success was not guaranteed. And I won. Setbacks couldn't stop me. They shouldn't stop you.

The conditions are never perfect. They are sometimes horrendous. But when an opportunity comes your way, none of that matters. All you have to do is take it.

"Prejudice won't deter me"

––––––––––––––––––––––

ROMAN RENTAL

It was spring 2000 and I was in one of the most beautiful cities in the world: Rome. It was my last six months as a trainee and I was working in the newly acquired Rome office of magic circle law firm Allen & Overy. On the day in question I took a taxi to a street I'd never seen before, which was surprising. I'd been walking this incredible city back and forth to the office two hours a day for three months and knew it like the back of my hand.

The taxi pulled up in front of one of the most beautiful terraces I've ever seen. Stunning ornate balconies, tall gleaming floor-to-ceiling windows and a terribly imposing but beautifully carved entrance door told me straight away that this was where money lived. Lots and lots of it. I remember thinking, not for the first time, who are these people? How do they get to live like this?

"But who is she?"

I was sitting on a sofa in a cavernous room opposite an elderly lady. Her hands were dripping with jewels and her angular, not altogether friendly-looking face was framed by silver sculptured hair. She reminded me of Miss Havisham, but after one of those TV makeovers that leave you not entirely sure whether the after shot is in fact an improvement or whether you preferred them the way they were. Next to me sat Melanie, a colleague from the office who had campaigned to find me somewhere better to live than the shoebox apartment in a dark, dingy street near Campo de' Fiori, which had been my home up to that point. That day we were meeting a potential new landlady. Melanie had played down this meeting, but I was grateful I had dressed for the occasion all the same. I am suited and booted and I look every inch the trustworthy lawyer from one of the most reputable law firms in the world. Or so I thought.

Melanie's platinum-blonde hair was tied back neatly into a ponytail and she too was smartly dressed. As PA to the office's managing partner, she knew how to represent the firm. The dormant artist in me thinks we must have been quite a beautiful sight sitting there in that ornately deco-rated room, the contrast of my black skin and shaved head next to her white skin and long blonde hair. But there was nothing beautiful about what happened next.

After sitting on that couch for 15 minutes I was still invis-ible. Miss Havisham literally looked through me. I spoke, but I was ignored. I tried to offer answers to her questions, but I was dismissed with the wave of a hand. Miss Hav-isham made no attempt to hide her shock at the sight of me, and her evident distaste at the thought of me. After a furtive glance in my direction, she leaned conspiratorially towards Melanie and repeated:

"Yes, but who is she? *Why is she* here?"

"But how did she get here?"

"Tell me, who brought her over and why is she *really* here?"

There was no eye contact. There was no communication with me at all. I became so angry I heard only fragments of Melanie's response. "Solicitor from the London office... Banking and capital markets... Here for six months, then returning to London. Yes, that's right, she's a lawyer. No, she's from London. No, not Africa. No, she is not illegal. No, she really is working as a lawyer. We have references. We are happy to provide extra guarantees..."

It finally dawned on me that this woman had completely misunderstood. I heard the words "Africa" and "boats" and "how long for?" and "who brought her over?" and I felt sick. And suddenly it takes me back to the day, a few weeks after starting my training seat in Rome, when I was sitting in a car in a line of traffic with my new colleagues (all white, naturally), and along the roadside was an end-less line of young black women, high heeled and scantily clad, enticing bored white drivers with the offer of a hun-dred ways they could help to alleviate their boredom. I thought about the comments I had become accustomed to getting as I walked down the street, and it hit me: the only other black people I'd seen in Rome were there, on the periphery of society, used, exploited, excluded. And suddenly I wasn't just the only one in that cavernous cold room, or in the office, I felt like the only one in the whole city. And the overwhelming message coming from the embodiment of whiteness, privilege and prejudice in front of me was, "You don't belong here. You are an imposter."

The apartment the firm rented – in their name, obviously, but on my behalf – was nothing short of incredible. I loved it because of its incredible location (I had a view of the Roman Forum from my bedroom window). But I loved it all the more because I knew how much Miss Havisham would have suffered knowing there was a black woman living in her apartment.

My reaction could have been different. When I recall the comments and even abuse that would be shouted at me in the street, and how seemingly educated people spoke about other cultures and ethnicities, I realise how easily I could have hated that city and never wanted to return. But I've been fighting these battles for years and I've learned how to win. Prejudice won't deter me. It shouldn't deter you.

"Exclusivity won't keep me out"

As a qualified banking lawyer at Allen & Overy, I was fortunate enough to have a decent boss. I was an eager, hard-working, head-down member of his team, almost always over-stretched but keeping myself afloat.

My boss and the more senior lawyers seemed to have client events and trips all the time. I would slog away into the early hours alone in the office, going home to top up on four or five hours' sleep, and then return to the office to overhear my boss in conversation with his senior team about the client event they attended the previous night and the upcoming golf trip they were planning the following week. I would listen to those conversations with curiosity and wonder, and I soon saw how significant those client events were. On the surface they looked like an excuse for a good time, the kind of fun that I assumed came with seniority and amazing things like expense accounts. But gradually, it dawned on me – these meetings on the golf course; the fancy restaurants and the drinking sessions that went on into the early hours – this is where much of the magic happened. It's where partners schmoozed their clients. It's where hands were shaken and deals were done. If you wanted to get ahead, that was where you had to be.

CLAY PIGEON SHOOTING

Eventually, I got lucky. Someone had dropped out of a client event at the last minute and a space was available. When my boss offered it to me, I was excited. But when I found out we were going clay pigeon shooting, I was nervous. I had never been clay pigeon shooting before. Before working in the corporate world, I'd never even heard of it. I had no idea what the right clothing was, but I knew I didn't have it because all I owned were suits for long hours in the office and jeans and jumpers for the weekend. As for my competence with shooting a shotgun: zero. All I had was a lazy right eye that refused to work, and an exhausted left eye that reluctantly picked up the slack.

It was a typically British rainy day. I was wearing trainers, jeans and a heavy woollen coat, which I remember, because standing in the cold holding a shotgun you don't know how to shoot while wearing a jacket, trousers and shoes that are not weatherproof is an experience that you don't forget. I was freezing. And I felt quite embarrassed to be standing next to a group of men fully decked out in Hunter boots and those big waxed jackets that everyone who lives in the country seems to wear. It was a scene straight out of Sherlock Holmes – all flat caps and tweed and leather patches. I was just waiting for someone to pull out a pipe.

As I've said, I'd never been shooting before, so I was nervous. But when I'm nervous, I talk. So I'm standing there, trying to look as if I know what I'm doing. The woman next to me is a client, so I do my best to look competent. Everybody raises their shotgun, takes aim and starts to fire. I raise mine, I look along the nose of it with my unreliable eyesight and, long after everyone else has lowered their shotguns and the pigeons are gone, I fire into the enormous expanse of grey that is the sky. I am not only clueless about this strange activity, I am utterly useless at it. I fail shot after shot, and watch as those around me "bravo" each other and egg each other on. In an attempt to stay positive and hide my embarrassment, I lean towards the client to my left and ask, "When are we going to shoot the real pigeons?"

She looks at me and her eyes say, "are you serious?". "We're not shooting real pigeons," she says making absolutely no attempt to hide her bemusement. "We're CLAY pigeon shooting." I was mortified. I felt totally humiliated. And you can bet I remained very quiet the rest of that day. When I replayed the day's events over in my mind the next day, the embarrassment surfaced. But so too did my pride. I refused to beat myself up for not having ever been clay shooting before. How many times had I been here, doing something for the first time, when those around me had been doing it all their lives? I've battled exclusivity my whole life and I know how to win.

Two years later, I went on secondment[9] to that same client as their banking lawyer. The woman who'd been so unimpressed by my ignorance that day wasn't there, but two of the men were and swore they had no recollection of me seeming out of place that day. Perhaps they had been far too busy focusing on their own performance to care about mine.

It could have been different. I could have been angry and resentful at the exclusive world of white privilege activities that make building relationships with clients an uneven playing field. I could have let it be the reason for me to withdraw, or to tell myself I don't stand a chance in a white world. But I didn't let that derail me. I stayed on track. Exclusivity couldn't keep me out. It shouldn't keep you out either.

Find your power

I've been fighting the battle against systemic bias my whole life. I've been the only one in the room, I've not fitted in. I've been prejudged and insulted and I've faced setbacks and challenges that the majority of my white peers did not encounter growing up. But I've found my power and I've fought those battles. And that's how I've won.

How are you showing up to your battles against racial bias? When those around you treat you like an imposter, what do you do? When they call you names, when they exclude you and are prejudiced against you, how do you react? Do you let it stop you? Do you let it hold you down or keep you out? Or do you play to win?

We've seen that when you're a person of colour in a white world Imposter Syndrome presents a unique challenge.

You don't just feel like an imposter, you're treated like one. But depending on those around you to change and waiting for a broken system to be fixed will leave you feeling powerless and make you a victim. You're handing all of the responsibility for your wellbeing, your success, your mental health and your career fulfilment to others, and retaining none for yourself. I don't accept this type of powerlessness, and neither should you. It's time to find your power.

Summary

»   Statistics shouldn't trap you.

»   Names shouldn't stop you.

»   Prejudice shouldn't deter you.

»   Setbacks shouldn't stop you.

»   Powerlessness shouldn't work for you.

»   Exclusivity shouldn't keep you out.

»   Don't accept powerlessness. It's time to find your power.

PART II

THE BATTLE AGAINST
SYSTEMIC BIAS

INTRODUCTION TO PART II

"If you don't like something, change it. If you can't change it, change your attitude."

– MAYA ANGELOU

I n Part I, you gained a deep understanding of Imposter Syndrome, why it affects you and how it is holding you back from progressing your career. We saw that although Imposter Syndrome affects the majority of people, your experience of Imposter Syndrome is different. Not only do you have to conquer self-doubt, you also have to triumph over systemic bias.

In Part II, I'm going to show you how to win the external battle against systemic bias. We'll look at how your thoughts about the systemic bias around you are making you powerless and are stifling your ability to navigate your way through it. You'll discover how to identify the situations and events that trigger negative reactions which hinder and limit you, and learn how to create a more positive outcome for yourself just by changing your thoughts.

We are starting with systemic bias because this is currently where most of your attention is. This is hardly surprising. When you encounter systemic bias in one form or another every day, it can be hard to think of much else. But it's also the easiest part for you to focus on because it's all happening outside of you. It's so much easier to complain about what others are doing wrong and how they should do things differently than it is to look inside and change yourself. But as long as your success depends on others changing, you'll always feel powerless. You can try to influence them, but you don't control them. However, you can control your own thoughts and actions, and this is how you get better results. Remember, we are not saying that the system doesn't need to be changed from the outside. We are taking our power back so we can progress all the way to leadership and change the system from the inside.

Until now, you've believed that the battle against systemic bias is a battle against how others treat you and how the system is flawed. You thought it was a battle for diversity, inclusion and authenticity and against racism. In Part II I'm going to show you that it isn't. It's a battle for your thoughts and your reactions to them. Systemic bias doesn't have to stop you. You can stop it holding you back by changing your reaction to it. This is how you take back your power and it's how you'll find a way to succeed.

THE DIVERSITY DISTRACTION

"If we let ourselves, we shall always be waiting for some distraction or other to end before we can really get down to our work."

– C.S. LEWIS

When you are a high potential person of colour, the lack of diversity in your organisation is palpable. As we've seen in Part I, it's almost impossible to forget. Every time you walk into a room and survey its occupants, that lack of diversity stares you in the face. It is, both literally and metaphorically, glaringly obvious.

Now I am going to introduce you to the Diversity Distraction – this is the belief that you can't succeed in a white world unless and until there is greater diversity in your organisation. I want you to set aside the beliefs that position you as a victim, so you can take back your power, triumph over bias and continue to fulfil your potential.

We'll look at how you respond to the lack of diversity around you and the impact you are allowing this to have on you personally. I'm going to show you that even though the lack of diversity in your organisation is, for all the reasons we have discussed, a barrier to your success, it doesn't have to stop you. I'm going to show you how to override it by managing your thoughts and your actions in response to it. By the end of this chapter, you'll be able to spot when you're falling victim to the Diversity Distraction, and you'll have the tools to help you step beyond it. As a result, the lack of diversity around you will no longer feel like a barrier to your success because you have the know-how to anticipate it and navigate your way around it, so you stay on track.

JESSICA'S STORY

I remember an unusually warm evening in late November of 2018 when I was standing outside one of London's most exclusive and beautiful hotels with my husband, Paul. We were there to attend a fundraiser ball for a charity we have supported as a family for over 10 years[10] and had arranged to meet my friend Jessica and her partner outside the venue before going in. Jessica is a 29-year-old banker with a Ghanaian father and an Ethiopian mother.

I've known Jessica since she attended one of my keynote talks at her bank three years ago. After the event, we had a long discussion about her Imposter Syndrome and the challenges she'd encountered being one of only three people of colour in her department. We stayed in touch and quickly became friends.

That evening, we were both in formal dress. Paul looked his usual dashing self in a black and navy Hugo Boss tux, and as usual, when I have an excuse to dress up, I was wearing Roland Mouret – a white strapless work of art I had bought the previous summer after the shop consultant told me it made me look like Halle Berry. When I looked at the reflection in the mirror that day, that's not who I saw staring back at me. But what did it matter if I didn't actually look like Halle Berry? That dress made me *feel like* Halle Berry! And what else matters?

Jessica arrived, her tiny birdlike frame dressed head to toe in emerald green, bold gold pendant earrings dangle from her ears, complementing the yellow tones in her skin. Her freshly braided hair twisted into curves and swirls across her head before snaking elegantly down her back to her waist. She looked absolutely stunning. I hug her like I mean it and excitedly we go in.

Ten minutes later we are standing in a group in a crowded ballroom of perhaps 200 people, feeling the buzzy excitement you get at the beginning of what you know is going to be a fantastic evening. There are chandeliers, free-flowing champagne and Christmas decorations adorning every table. Everything sparkles. It's beautiful.

I turn to say something to Jessica but her face tells me she is not feeling it.

"This is so frustrating!" She shouts the words into my ear in part to be heard, and in part to show the extent of her frustration.

"Why does it always have to be this way? Why are we always the only ones in the room?"

Jessica was right. There it was: the sea of white faces. Of course, I'd seen it the moment I entered the room. There was no shortage of people like us serving the champagne, but there was no one like us drinking it.

Less than an hour later, I left the table to head for the bathroom and motioned Jessica to follow me. We weren't sitting next to each other, so I wanted to check in and see if she was having a good time. "It's so damn white in here. I can't stand it," Jessica said. "I know. And I get it," I replied. "But are you managing to meet some people? Are you networking? I hope you're networking!" I said, keeping the mood light and keen to remind Jessica of one of her main reasons for being there. "I have been,

"

There was no shortage of people like us serving the champagne, but there was no one like us drinking it.

"

but what's the point?" Jessica responded. "These events are all the same. The people are the same. Nothing's ever going to change. Seriously, doesn't it depress you? I think about it all the time and it really gets me down."

"But we're not the only ones, Jessica. We're the first!"

Since that night, I've coached Jessica on how to progress her career at the bank. It may not surprise you to hear that the focus of our session was on Jessica's struggles with being the only one in the room. After some exploration, it became clear just how damaging this mindset was proving to be for her. The "what's the point?" attitude that had hijacked her enjoyment of that ball was also impacting her performance and enjoyment of her work. Jessica was going to fewer and fewer work events, and when she did attend, she would always stick to the small circle of people she already knew. When she received negative feedback, she treated it as further proof that she would never get ahead in a place where "nobody gets me". One of the negative outcomes of this was that Jessica had been sending the message to those around her that she wasn't particularly ambitious and had no interest in getting promoted. It was a complete surprise to Jessica's boss when, during her annual review, Jessica asked about her prospects for promotion.

Thankfully, as a result of our work together, Jessica started to see how the way she had been thinking about and responding to the problem had kept her stuck. I helped her to shift from being frustrated by the lack of diversity in her organisation to being motivated by it.

Jessica still notices the sea of white faces around her. But as a result of our work together, she knows how to manage her thoughts and reactions in a way that produces a much better outcome for her. When her mind wants to think "what's the point?" and "why am I the only one?", she knows now this is a distraction. That it can keep her stuck, but it doesn't have to. She remembers my advice to focus on why she is in the room and what she is there to do. Jessica is going through the promotion application process at the bank this year. Even without knowing the outcome of her application, the fact that Jessica was able and willing to apply for a role that would embed her into senior management as the only black face, illustrates just how far Jessica has come.

Are you, like Jessica, distracted by the lack of diversity around you? Have you ever found yourself the only person of colour in the room and felt so frustrated by it that it distracted you both from what you were there to do and from the longer-term goal you had set out to achieve? Do you ever show up to work feeling so despondent about the way things are that you start to question the point of you being there?

HOW TO SPOT THE DIVERSITY DISTRACTION

It's easy to fall into this trap. How many of these sound like you?

- You see the lack of diversity everywhere in your organisation and are always talking about it.

- You often refer to the lack of role models who look like you and take this as evidence you'll never succeed.

- You cite the lack of diversity in your organisation as proof that the only way you can progress is to move somewhere else.

- You regularly attend events and talks that spend more time focusing on the problem than they do on discussing the solution.

- You're thinking about leaving because you're tired of being the only one in the room.

- You have never stopped to consider that by focusing on your own development, in spite of the lack of diversity around you, you can be part of the solution.

How the Diversity Distraction keeps you stuck

When you think about the lack of diversity around you, the natural response is to think you don't stand a chance. It seems inevitable that you'll never progress or succeed because, as is evident from the all-white leadership, people like you don't get ahead in places like this. But is it?

"Distraction is the only thing that consoles us for miseries and yet it is itself the greatest of our miseries,"

- BLAISE PASCAL

The problem with thinking you'll never succeed or progress is it keeps you stuck. It sets off a chain reaction that starts with you feeling powerless and ends with you reducing your chances of getting the results you are looking for. Here's how it works:

1. You feel powerless, resentful and frustrated

The lack of diversity around you is out of your direct control. When we focus on something we can't control we feel powerless in the face of it. This leaves you feeling frustrated with the way things are, and resentful towards those around you who perpetuate or benefit from the status quo.

2. Your confirmation bias is activated

If you believe that the lack of diversity around you means you will never succeed or get ahead, your brain will set out to prove it. In psychology, this is known as "confirmation bias". It's when your brain subconsciously looks for evidence that will confirm what you already believe to be true. Therefore, if you believe you can't get ahead because you're the only one in the room, your clever brain will be highly selective about the information it allows in. It will deliberately seek out evidence from all around you that supports this belief and ignore any evidence in front of you that would contradict it. Not only does this reinforce your feeling of powerlessness, it also guarantees that you'll be blind to any opportunities for success that come your way.

3. You self-sabotage

The feeling of powerlessness your thinking creates has a damaging effect because your emotions dictate how you show up. Think about how you perform a simple task like putting the bins out for collection the next morning (nobody's favourite job, and one I have delegated to my teenage boys!). Think about how you'd perform that task if you were feeling positive and motivated. Now consider how you'd perform that same task if you were feeling powerless and resentful. In each case, the task is the same, but how you perform and, by extension, the outcome you create is different. When you think negatively, you show up from a negative place and sabotage your chances of getting the results you want.

4. You block your own resourcefulness

When you're focused on the lack of diversity around you, it's easy to forget all the resources and skills you have at your disposal for dealing with the situation at hand. Human beings have certain innate abilities. We are hard-wired for survival. This means we are creative and adaptive; we can communicate, plan, influence and solve problems; and we are resilient. These are the innate resources you were born with. The fact that you are where you are today demonstrates not only how well you have developed and applied these resources successfully in the past but also your capacity to do so in the future. But these resources are all blocked when your attention is diverted outside of you to the things around you which you have no direct control over.

5. You create the result you wanted to avoid

Thinking that you'll never get ahead until the diversity problem is fixed may become a self-fulfilling prophecy. Can you see how, by showing up from a feeling of powerlessness, sabotaging yourself and getting in your own way by blocking your resourcefulness, the most likely outcome is that you struggle to get ahead and succeed? Your thoughts about the lack of diversity around you are producing the very outcome you've been trying to avoid.

How to sidestep the Diversity Distraction

The only way to sidestep the lack of diversity in your organisation, so that it doesn't keep you stuck, is to change your response to it. You do this by anticipating the situations in which it's likely to occur and then when it does, choosing a response that will help you stay on track.

What triggers me?

Ask yourself: when I feel conscious of being the only one in the room, where am I? What brings on my frustration about the lack of diversity in my organisation? Is it a comment? A certain situation? Is it when I'm interacting with a particular person? For example, it could be that every time you attend a team meeting you are struck by the visual that is a sea of white faces. Or perhaps it's every time the newly promoted partners in your firm are announced and you see that all of them are white. It could even be just walking into the office each day! These are your triggers – the circumstances which trigger you to respond or react in a certain way. React one way, and the lack of diversity is a barrier that will keep you stuck. Respond differently, and you get to go around it.

How do I normally react?

The second step to changing your response then, is to understand your default reaction when a trigger event occurs.

Your default reaction is a chain of events that involves your thoughts, emotions, actions and results. The secret to side-stepping the Diversity Distraction is understanding that it's your thoughts that produce your emotions, and that it's these emotions that determine your actions and it's your actions that are responsible for your results.

You can see this at work in Jessica's case. Constantly thinking "what's the point?" (her thought) made her feel powerless and despondent (emotion). Because she felt powerless and despondent, she had been showing up to work and work-related events half-heartedly (her actions), which sent the message to her seniors that she was neither ready for nor interested in a promotion (the result: she stays stuck).

What thoughts go through your mind when you are triggered? Perhaps your thought is: "why am I always the only one?" Or maybe your thought is: "you can only get ahead in this place if you're white" or "I'll never be respected in a place where all the leaders are white."

Once you have identified your typical thought pattern, you can work through the chain:

- How do these thoughts make me feel? (emotion)

- How am I showing up when I feel like this? (emotion)

- What am I doing/not doing as a result? (action)

- What results am I creating? (results)

How can I change my response?

The way I helped Jessica to change her response was with simple but powerful coaching questions that interrupted her default thought pattern and helped her see the same situation in a different light. Instead of thinking, "Why am I always the only one?" at her group meetings, one of Jessica's new thoughts was "What am I here to do?". As a result of thoughts like this, Jessica gradually went from feeling powerless and despondent in these meetings to feeling determined and focused, which meant she was able to show up in a completely different way. This is how you sidestep the Diversity Distraction.

"I don't focus on what I'm up against. I focus on my goals and I try to ignore the rest."

- VENUS WILLIAMS

Below are examples of coaching questions you can use to help change your response to the lack of diversity around you. When a trigger event occurs, ask yourself:

- What did I come here to do?

- Who else is in the room?

- What am I assuming?

- Where do I want to focus my attention today?

- If I knew I was the first of many in the room, what would I do?

- Who do I want to be today?

- Where's the opportunity here?

- How do I want to show up to this?

What does this bring up for you?

If the idea that you should have to work this hard to overcome the lack of diversity around you bothers you then you're not alone. I've felt that exact same frustration myself in the past. There have been times when I've thought: Why me? Why should I have to be the one to change my attitude? Why not them? But all these feelings ever did was make me feel worse. I learned that changing my thinking was the more empowered choice. I wasn't wishing things were different and waiting for the world to change. Neither was I ignoring the problem. I was side-stepping it so that I could stay on track, stay focused on progressing my career, which would allow me to eventually become part of the solution. By following these steps, you can create this outcome for yourself too.

THE WHITEST RESTAURANT

I'm walking through a part of London I rarely go to, from Tottenham Court Road to Charing Cross. It's a beautiful day, and such a treat to be walking. My feet are a little sore, but that's my own fault. Despite the call for women to free themselves from the tyranny of high heeled shoes, I still insist on wearing my suede 3-inch pumps.

This is London's West End, the thriving busy heart of one of the most cosmopolitan cities in the world. Walk down the street at any time of day and you'll encounter people of all ages, colours and styles.

The National Portrait Gallery, which claims to be the home to over 195,000 portraits of historically important and famous British people, is housed in an impressive building on St Martin's Place. As I enter the large imposing entrance, I glance at my watch to double-check I am on time for lunch. I feel a rush of excitement when I realise that I'm 20 minutes early for lunch with my client Emily, and that the finalists in this year's annual BP Portrait Award are on exhibit in the room to my right.

The paintings on display – a cornucopia of faces, figures and features of all shapes and sizes, colours and shades – take my breath away. They are so diverse, so richly detailed that they come alive before my eyes. I feel the flicker of remorse and longing for the 16-year-old Caroline who reluctantly gave up art after GCSE level. But there is plenty here that speaks to the passion for history that I pursued all the way to degree level before my transition to law.

One painting in particular catches my eye. When I research the painting a few days later, I discover it's called "A throne in the West" by an Italian called Massimiliano Pironti[11]. But on the day in question, I see only the painting: a portrait of a young black woman on a chair. She is wearing blue jeans and a light patterned shirt. Her hair is braided. Her skin is a deep brown. She sits casually with one knee raised and her feet are bare. She is staring straight at me, and I'm staring back at her, wondering what she is thinking. But before I can work it out, a glance at the clock tells me it's time to go.

Emily and I are meeting to celebrate her brilliant promotion to Director and the fact she is now one of the first and only senior black women directors in London in an organisation of over 500 partners and directors. Emily had reached out to me for coaching when she discovered she was being put forward for promotion. She wanted to ensure she presented her best possible case for promotion and, like so many of my clients, saw the value of investing in her own professional development. Our coaching sessions covered a range of topics, but central to all of them was what it meant to be the only black candidate, and to be stepping into leadership where she will continue to be the only one in the room. Emily still tells me how much the work she did with me changed her. The work we did on how she shows up, how she views herself and her goals and purpose, created a huge shift away from being the only one in the room to being unique, valuable and a trailblazer.

I take the escalators to the restaurant on the top floor of the gallery and give my name. The woman at the entrance is formal but smiley and shows me to my seat. As I follow her to our table I'm dazzled by the brightness of the room. I'm in a rooftop restaurant with glass panelling and it's an unusually sunny day in London. The sun beams through the windows and I think how bright everything is.

And then I look around, and I note with a slight jolt how white everyone is.

There's a flicker of surprise as I register that I'm the only one in the room. My mind jumps momentarily back to the streets outside, and to the room downstairs with its striking, arresting portraits, and I'm stunned by the contrast. I think of the young black woman in the Pironti painting and wonder how she would feel in this room. Would the lack of diversity distract? Would she allow it to throw her off track?

A wave of white heads turns in unison to look at me. Their looks aren't overtly hostile, but they express enough curiosity and surprise to trigger a momentary feeling of self-consciousness. Was it the sound of my heels on the stone floor that drew their attention or my bright pink coat? No, everyone in the room can see what I see: the stark contrast of my black skin against the backdrop of this gleaming, white restaurant. Sometimes you just know.

Emily arrives. Like me, she loves colour. As she floats over to our table dressed head-to-toe in sapphire blue, all hair extensions and beautiful full smile, a wave of white heads rises and falls again. Emily and I hug, exchange smiles and, as our eyes meet, the expression on our faces says it all. "Could this restaurant be any whiter?" I whisper conspiratorially. "I don't think they got the diversity memo," she replies, and we both laugh. "I think we need to come here more often, Emily. We need to help shake things up a bit."

The lack of diversity around you is going to take some time to fix. The good news is you don't have to stand by feeling powerless waiting for the system to change. You can sidestep this barrier by changing your response to it.

The old powerless you, the you that feels like a victim as the only person of colour in your working world, will want to resist this. You'll tell yourself this is letting your organisation and an unequal system off the hook. It isn't. What it is doing is putting you on the hook too. It's saying you have a role to play and a contribution to make, and the best way you can do that is to find your power.

Finding your power when the lack of diversity is all around you isn't easy. You'll need to be courageous and resilient and be willing to persevere. You'll need a goal to keep you motivated and a purpose to drive you. The good news is that you already have these resources within you. I'm going to give you the tool to help you access these in Part III.

Summary

» As a person of colour striving to succeed in a white world, there will be times when you'll feel isolated and alone.

» But beware of the "Diversity Distraction" – the belief that you can't get ahead until the lack of diversity in your organisation has been fixed.

» The battle to succeed in a world where few people look like you is a battle you can win!

» Identify specific circumstances in which your diversity fear is triggered.

» When you feel isolated and alone, challenge your thinking and consider your options.

» Be intentional in how you respond by choosing a response that serves you.

THE INCLUSION ILLUSION

*"No one can make you feel inferior
without your consent."*

- ELEANOR ROOSEVELT

As a high potential person of colour battling to succeed in a white world, you know what it's like not to feel included. As we've seen in Part I, getting through the door doesn't exactly open up a clear route to success. When there are unwritten rules you're not aware of, and inner circles you feel excluded from, just being in the room isn't enough.

In this chapter, we are looking at thoughts you are having around how excluded you feel and your belief that you need someone else to include you in order to get ahead. I call this belief the Inclusion Illusion because it seduces you into thinking that if no one is including you, you are powerless to do anything about it. The lack of inclusiveness in your organisation is indeed a barrier to your progress. But, as with the lack of diversity around you, it doesn't have to stop you. I'm going to show you how to sidestep it by managing your thoughts and your actions in response to it. As a result, you'll be able to spot when you're being seduced by the Inclusion Illusion, and you'll have the tools to help you step beyond it. You'll realise that when you are aware of the Inclusion Illusion, can anticipate it and have the tools to navigate around it, the battle to succeed in a non-inclusive world is a battle you can win.

MANJIT'S STORY

When I met Manjit, he had already been a victim of the Inclusion Illusion. I found myself having a coaching conversation with him when our professional paths crossed at a networking event last year. The challenge he faced as a person of colour in the predominantly white firm where he worked is a great example of the Inclusion Illusion at work. Manjit is a tall, striking man with piercing eyes and (I couldn't help noticing) an abundance of facial hair. He is not much of a small talker, so I quickly learned from our conversation that he was born in London to Indian parents who moved to the UK in the '50s. No one in his family drinks alcohol, and he is no exception. Manjit qualified as a Mergers and Acquisitions (M&A) lawyer at one of the City law firms as part of a graduate intake that was, initially at least, 46% BAME (Black, Asian or of Minority Ethnic origin) as classified by the firm. It was a buoyant time for the mergers and acquisitions market, and Manjit thought his biggest challenge would be coping with the punishingly long hours in the office his firm's M&A clients demanded, but he soon discovered that this was the least of his problems. The real challenge, it turned out, was not all the long nights he had spent drafting agreements in the office. It was the late nights on the town. Manjit felt under constant pressure to go for drinks and dinner at which vast amounts of alcohol were consumed into the early hours.

According to Manjit, he'd started out with a positive attitude and the best of intentions. As a trainee, it was relatively easy to be selective about what social events he attended, and when he felt the pressure or that it was the right thing to do, he would turn up to these events, but not drink. He usually found a way to slip away quietly when people had had enough drinks not to notice, and before things became too unruly and messy.

It was during his early years as an associate that Manjit started to find things hard. Now the social events weren't just internal and at his level. They were broader, with more senior lawyers and partners in attendance and, increasingly, some of the firm's biggest clients. Manjit's strategy of showing up for a few glasses of watered-down orange juice and slipping away quietly no longer worked. It happened gradually at first, but soon became impossible to ignore. He felt a growing sense of exclusion, that he didn't belong. This caused him to feel more and more withdrawn, even though that wasn't his intention. He started to worry that he just wasn't social enough to stay.

"It seems such a stupid thing, to leave your job because you don't drink and everyone around you does," I recall him saying. "But it slowly gnaws away at you. I kept getting that feeling that it was all happening without me and I hated that feeling. I resented seeing average lawyers who were part of the in-crowd getting first dibs on the interesting deals. It had nothing to do with whether I was a good lawyer or not. What it boiled down to was my credentials as a drinker."

For Manjit, what had been a cultural norm for him his whole life, turned out to be the nail in the coffin of his legal career. He concluded that the pervasive drinking culture was so fundamental to progressing to leadership at the firm, he had zero chance of making it. Leaving, he felt, was the only choice he had.

It was too late for me to help Manjit save his career as a private practice lawyer, as this had all taken place before we'd met. But it wasn't too late for me to challenge his thinking about how powerless he had been when he felt excluded. I discovered that "the not drinking thing" had been an issue for Manjit long before he joined his last firm. Throughout university and law school, it had been a barrier to him really connecting with those who didn't share his cultural values around drinking. In the short conversation I had, it was easy to identify the events or comments that would trigger Manjit's frustration. And each time he would become defensive and withdraw. I did two things for Manjit. I suggested to him that the feeling of exclusion that had followed him around since university would not go away and would most likely follow him around his whole career. Then I offered Manjit a different viewpoint: the idea he needed others to include him was an illusion that was keeping him stuck. If he wasn't being included, what he needed to do was to include himself.

Have you ever felt the frustration of not fitting in because the behaviour of those around you is so alien to you? Have you, like Manjit, felt less valued and respected, not because of the quality of your work, but because you don't have the same values as your white peers or seniors? Does this make you question whether you're in the right place or, worse still, have you decided to leave a previous job because of this?

HOW TO SPOT THE INCLUSION ILLUSION

It's easy to be seduced by the Inclusion Illusion. How many of these do you connect with?

- Whether it's an event, a dinner, a lunch or a meeting, you always wait to be invited, you never do the inviting.

- You resent being asked to explain cultural references to white people who don't understand (in the black community, this is known as "blacksplaining").

- You avoid attending events which, while commonplace in a white corporate world, you have no prior experience of.

- You are quick to dismiss events you have not been exposed to growing up because you associate them with white privilege.

- You are angered by the number of white privilege events in your organisation's client calendar.

- You frequently bemoan how un-inclusive your organisation is.

- You're rigid and strict about what you are or aren't prepared to do.

How the Inclusion Illusion keeps you stuck

The problem with thinking that others need to invite you in order for you to succeed is that it keeps you stuck. It certainly feels good to be invited by someone else. It's nice when you feel someone is thinking of you, making the effort on your behalf and not behaving in a way that excludes you. But when the invitation isn't forthcoming, and the effort isn't being made, sitting around waiting for someone to show up doesn't help you. It leaves you feeling like a victim and, just as with the Diversity Distraction, it blinds you to your power. Here's how:

1. You feel powerless, resentful and frustrated

How prepared others are to include you is out of your direct control. Therefore, focusing on this and wishing things were different just leaves you powerless. As in Manjit's case, you'll feel increasingly frustrated and resentful of those who you feel should be including you but aren't. The problem with this type of thinking is it leaves you feeling powerless and resentful and this is a dangerous place to show up from. When you're resentful you're likely to withdraw. You'll do less and less and send signals that you don't want to be included.

2. Your confirmation bias is activated

Remember the confirmation bias we talked about in relation to the Diversity Distraction? It works exactly the same way with the Inclusion Illusion. As long as you think that career progression is only possible if others include you, your brain will go searching for the evidence to prove it's true, ignoring any signs or opportunities that might indicate otherwise.

3. You self-sabotage

Feeling powerless, resentful and/or frustrated is going to make things challenging during those moments when you feel you're being excluded because of how these emotions will show up. You're more likely to withdraw or avoid certain events or situations altogether. Even if you do make the effort to be involved, the negative emotions you have around the lack of inclusion may stifle your ability to contribute and show your value.

4. You block your own resourcefulness

You have so many internal resources available to you – your resilience, courage, your ability to persuade and influence, for example – that you could put to work in situations where you feel excluded. But if you're fully focused on the exclusion and the need for someone else to fix it, you'll block your access to these resources.

5. You create the result you wanted to avoid

You want to feel included and equal, but your negative thoughts around how others are excluding you could backfire because of the emotions they produce. Can you see that when you show up to events or situations, or even a normal day in the office, feeling powerless and frustrated because you're not included, it affects your interactions with others, the messages you send and how you perform? You might be more withdrawn or lacking in enthusiasm, for example. Those around you may then misinterpret your frustration as a sign that you don't want to be included, creating the very result you want to avoid.

How to sidestep the Inclusion Illusion

I've heard the lack of inclusion described as like being invited to the party but no one inviting you to dance. This sounds like a great metaphor for your experience of being excluded, but it's an even better metaphor for what you can do to change it. I'm a person who loves to dance. Put me in a room, play a half-decent tune and nothing will keep me off the dance floor. So I tried to imagine being invited to a party and having to wait to be asked to dance. And I didn't like it. I didn't like it one single bit. When I go to a party, I don't wait to be invited onto the dancefloor, I invite myself. This often means dancing on my own, so I usually feel a little self-conscious at first. But then I start to relax and get into it and I'm so busy being myself I don't worry who everybody else is being. My confidence grows. But it's not a defensive confidence which shuts people out, it's an open confidence that invites them in. It's a confidence that comes from being present with where I am and remembering why I am there. It also comes from being willing to show people who I am and not wait for them to ask or expect them to already know. Seeing my self-assurance, others join in and before I know it, I've started something, and I'm in the middle of it.

It doesn't happen every time. Sometimes when the music stops, I'm still dancing on my own (which, by the way, I love to do). But other times, it's incredible. I'll be on the dancefloor being myself, dancing the way *I* dance. And everywhere around me, people aren't just dancing, they are trying to dance like *me*.

The way you sidestep the Inclusion Illusion is to include yourself. How you do this is first, by understanding the situations in which you feel excluded (the trigger) and then being intentional in your response to it. Here is a strategy to help you do that:

What triggers me?

Ask yourself: when I feel I am not being included, where am I? What is going on? Is it a comment? A certain situation? Does it always happen when I'm in a group, or is there a particular person who makes me feel I'm excluded? Is it because of what happens in the office as part of a typical working day, or is it usually after work when we go elsewhere? Is it what people say that makes me feel excluded, or what people do? For example, it could be that white people in your group like to call each other by their last names. You know this is common amongst people who went to private school, and because you didn't, every time they address each other in this way, you feel excluded from the banter, and you feel that you'll never fit in with the group (you can't change where you went to school). It's important to be as specific as possible because these are your triggers – the circumstances which make you feel excluded. The better you are at spotting them, the more control you have over your reaction to them.

How do I normally react?

How do you typically react when a trigger event occurs? What's your default response?

You know from the Diversity Distraction that your default reaction is a chain of events that involves your thoughts, emotions, actions and results. The key to bypassing the Inclusion Illusion is understanding that it's your thoughts that produce your emotions, and that it's these emotions that determine your actions and it's your actions that are responsible for your results. To understand how this works in practice, let's think back to Minesh.

One of Minesh's triggers was going out for boozy drinks with the team or with clients. His default reaction was to think: "Why can't they make these decisions in the office when I'm around? They know I don't want to go out drinking and yet they continue to do it. It's as if they deliberately want to exclude me" (thoughts). These thoughts made Minesh feel frustrated and resentful (emotion). So now, because Minesh is showing up to work feeling frustrated and resentful, he says "whatever" when he is invited out, preferring instead to put his head down and just get the job done. This sends the message to those around him that he's not interested in fitting in, and they stop inviting him. The very situation Minesh was trying to avoid is perpetuated and the cycle repeats itself.

What thoughts go through your mind when you are triggered? Perhaps your thought is: "Why is it always the same group of people?" Or maybe your thought is "they never invite me" or "they only rate you if you've been to public school". Or perhaps it's that all the client events revolve around sports or experiences you were not exposed to growing up, like golf. Remember my clay pigeon experience? Have you experienced something similar?

Once you have identified your typical thought pattern, you can work through the chain:

- How do these thoughts make me feel? (emotion)

- How am I showing up when I feel like this? (emotion)

- What am I doing/not doing as a result of feeling like this? (action)

- What results am I creating? (results)

How can I change my response?

The way to sidestep the Inclusion Illusion is the same way you sidestepped the Diversity Distraction: you can do this by being more intentional about your thoughts when you're triggered, so that the resulting emotions you feel and action you then take, create a better result.

DIONE'S STORY

Dione was born in Ghana and moved to the UK with her parents when she was eight years old. At the age of 29, she found herself with a foot in the door of one of the biggest financial institutions in the City. After six years of what she calls "complete absorption" into her work, Dione had already acquired the experience and reputation of an expert in her field, and as a rising star. But, despite this increase in her experience level and the recognition she was getting internally, Dione noticed that her visibility in front of clients was stunted. Whenever clients who she worked for were in town or in-person meetings were organised, Dione was often the last to know. At first, she assumed this was a seniority issue, but soon began to notice that another colleague was being invited to attend regular meetings in her place. Not only was he white, male and three years her junior, but he was also the one who reported to her and for whom she had acted as a mentor throughout the three years he had been at the company. She couldn't believe it. Her boss would prefer to take her junior white colleague to client events rather than her.

Dione did not waste time wallowing in her exclusion and victimhood. She could have got stuck on the thought, "They're deliberately excluding me because I'm black. I'm never going to get ahead." Instead, her thoughts went straight to: "How can I get around this? Who do I know?" One of her clients came to mind. She met him for coffee and made it clear that she wanted to start attending the client meetings. Gradually, Dione was able to reinstate herself as the client's main contact.

Below are examples of coaching questions you can use to help you change your negative thoughts around the lack of inclusion around you. When a trigger event occurs, ask yourself:

- What am I resisting?

- What am I making this situation mean?

- How can I turn this into an opportunity?

- What can I bring to the table that no one else has?

- What other options do I have?

- Who am I being right now?

- What can I learn from this?

What does this bring up for you?

At first, you may hate the idea of having to include your-self. I did at first too. Memories of always being on the edge of the group at school, not to mention my injured sense of pride, caused me to think: I'm not going to ask. If they don't want me, that's fine. You may have had similar feelings. But this isn't school, this is your career. You have some responsibility for making it work and there's so much at stake. As systemic bias is not in a hurry to fix itself, it needs a little help from you.

What I'm asking you to do is hard. You'll need the moti-vation to dance through the initial loneliness and the resilience to keep trying when you don't get immediate results. I know exactly how to help you do this and I'll be showing you in Part III. But before we get to that, I need to alert you to the Authenticity Trap.

Summary

———————————————————————————————

» As a person of colour striving to succeed in a white world, there will be times when you'll feel excluded.

» But beware the "Inclusion Illusion" – the belief that inclusion only happens when someone else chooses to include you.

» The battle to succeed in a world which doesn't always include you is a battle you can win.

» Identify specific circumstances in which your inclusion fear is triggered.

» When you feel excluded, challenge your thinking and consider your options.

» Be intentional in how you respond by choosing a response that serves you.

THE AUTHENTICITY TRAP

*"Authenticity is about being true
to who you are."*

- MICHAEL JORDAN

As a high potential person of colour battling to succeed in a white world, most likely you've felt torn at times, between what is being asked of you if you want to succeed, and what feels authentic or a reflection of your true self. This is possibly because of your cultural heritage. As we've seen in Part I, people of colour in mostly white organisations often face cultural norms that are either unfamiliar or, even if they are familiar, are at odds with their upbringing or values. When your eligibility for promotion or the next big opportunity depends on a change in your style or behaviour, it can feel as though your authenticity is under threat.

The importance of authenticity to our mental health and performance in the workplace is well documented. We all recognise the significance of being able to be our true selves. But what does it mean to be your "true self", and where do you draw the line between your true self and the part of you that wants or needs to grow? The threat to authenticity in the workplace may well be real, but I'm here to warn you about another threat: the threat to fulfilling your potential. I call this threat the Authenticity Trap.

The Authenticity Trap is the belief that if progressing your career and succeeding in a white world requires a change in your behaviour, attitude or style, any such change would amount to a betrayal of your true self. This belief is not without cause. Being told that you should change the way you behave so that it is more palatable or acceptable to others, or to develop certain qualities in order to comply with an accepted norm, feels like a dangerous assault on who you are because it is one – the suggestion being that you be less "you" and more "them".

At other times, however, the threat is more perceived than real because it stems from your beliefs about what it takes to succeed in an all-white culture, and what it means to be true to yourself. When these beliefs go unchallenged, you risk falling into the trap of turning down opportunities to grow that would honour a part of your authentic self you have been ignoring or discounting.

It's time to take a look at the thoughts you have when someone asks you to change or suggests that you do something differently. I'm going to show you that this doesn't have to be a threat to your authenticity, and it doesn't have to stop you. You can transcend these suggestions and recommendations the same way you can transcend the lack of diversity and the lack of inclusion: by managing your thinking around each situation and choosing a response that serves you. I will show you how to spot the Authenticity Trap, and help you develop the awareness and the tools to avoid it, so that you'll no longer have to choose between being authentic and progressing your career. You'll find a way to have both.

SHARON'S STORY

When Sharon, a senior manager at a large tech company, reached out to me for coaching she was very specific about her objectives. Two of her peers had been promoted and she was furious. She felt certain it was because she wasn't the right "type". She had her own unique style of dress, and her own unique way of – in her words – "saying it like it is". Sharon wanted me to help her build up her CV and prepare for moving somewhere that "values me for who I am and isn't trying to turn me into someone I'm not".

We had a clear place to start in our coaching sessions: who exactly was she? After just one session exploring this question, I noticed a very distinct pattern in the way Sharon spoke about herself. She repeatedly used expressions like "that's just not me" and "I'm not one of those people who..." It soon became clear that Sharon had a very strong sense of identity. So strong you could say it was extremely rigid. She was very clear about the type of person she was and the type of person she wasn't.

My concern for Sharon was that she would find another job that seemed like the right fit initially, only to receive further negative feedback on her communication style and find herself back to square one: feeling that she wasn't valued for who she was and that no one would let her be herself. I told Sharon what I could see: she had fallen into the trap of interpreting suggestions that she improve her communication skills as an attack on her authenticity. I suggested that before she rushed out to start again in another job, we do some work together to explore what it meant to her to be authentic.

It was clear from the work we did together that what Sharon saw as authentic behaviour had evolved over time unconsciously, and somewhat haphazardly. Sharon had arrived at her sense of self the way most of us do: not as the result of a clearly considered set of principles and behaviours; but rather as a result of unconsciously acquired beliefs, lived experiences, adopted behaviours and cultural and environmental influences – all assimilated and absorbed over time. Some of the behaviours Sharon had decided to fix her authenticity to had become a rigid part of her identity simply because that was the way she had always done things. Sharon had not allowed for the fact that, for example, she was no longer a little girl with four older brothers who only took her seriously or heard her when she was abrupt and direct. Previously, Sharon's outspoken frankness had never been a problem. On the contrary, it had actually served her. But now she was poised to move up the career ladder into leadership, her style of communication was no longer effective.

At a certain point in our coaching, it became clear that Sharon had just become so used to thinking and behaving and dressing in a certain way, and that by default it had become "this is the way I am" and "this is the way I do things". When Sharon started receiving feedback on her behaviour skills, she felt her identity was under threat. When told that clients found her too confrontational, Sharon viewed this as a threat to a personal quality that not everybody likes, but that she had always been proud of: her ability to call it like it is and say things that others are too chicken to say.

Even when your authenticity is the result of positive reinforcement from home and strong cultural values, it still

"

To hold on too tightly to who we are is like holding on to a shoe that you can still squeeze into, but no longer fits.

"

needs to be adaptive. What you've adopted from tradition and learned from past experience cannot always be cut and pasted into new circumstances and won't always get you where you want to be. Principles and core values hold, but the way these are expressed and communicated and honoured can (and may need to) change without constituting a betrayal.

The most powerful work I did with Sharon was to help her see that being authentic did not mean there were aspects of her personality that she couldn't or shouldn't change. Her personality wasn't fixed, and it never had been. It was constantly evolving. As a result of our work together Sharon was able to see that she could improve her communication skills and still hold on to her value of being honest and saying what no one else would say, but that she could present this in a way that would make it easier for others to receive and learn from.

Sharon also made another important discovery: that her identity, and what she considered made her authentic, was not fixed in stone. She was able to recognise that her identity isn't fixed when she was born, it takes shape over time and it evolves in response to your environment – and environments change. Coaching helped her to see what is the human experience and our biggest challenge – to be in a world that is constantly changing, and to find our place in that new world as it does. To hold on too tightly to who we are is like holding on to a shoe that you can still squeeze into, but no longer fits.

Can you relate to Sharon's experience? Do you struggle to "be who you are" in the office and feel this is a barrier to your getting ahead? Have you ever found yourself refusing to adopt new behaviours because you feel they are simply "not how I am"? You may even have shied away from an opportunity for a promotion because you couldn't see yourself in the new role.

HOW TO SPOT THE AUTHENTICITY TRAP

Look honestly at yourself and see how many of these statements are true:

- You are defensive when you receive negative feedback about your behaviour.

- You use expressions like "I would never" or "that's just not me".

- You make reference to your way of doing things.

- You feel it's impossible to be yourself.

- You think you're the same person you've always been.

- You question the authenticity and integrity of those ahead of you.

- You are determined to not let success or progression change you.

How the Authenticity Trap keeps you stuck

When asked to change or adapt your behaviour in order to succeed (for example, to be considered for promotion), the obvious response is to feel that you can't be true to yourself at work if you want to get ahead. It seems logical to read any suggestion that you adapt your communication style, change your leadership style or alter the way you present yourself as a threat to your true self. But is it?

This type of thinking keeps you stuck. This is because being focused on holding onto your authenticity can trap you into thinking that your identity is fixed, and that doing things differently would be a betrayal of who you are. A rigid idea of what constitutes authentic behaviour limits you to a narrow set of rules that leave no room for you to evolve and grow as your circumstances, environment and goals change. When you resist any suggestion that you change (the way you communicate or deliver feedback to others, for example) because you perceive it as a threat to your authenticity, the following negative chain reaction is likely to occur:

1. You feel powerless, resentful and frustrated

Elevating all your traits, styles and behaviours to the status of "identity critical" leaves you nowhere to go when it feels as though these are under attack. You can't progress unless you change. But you can't change because what's at stake (your identity) is too important. This catch-22 leaves you feeling powerless, resentful and deeply frustrated with the way things are.

2. Your confirmation bias is activated

As we've seen, because your brain likes to be efficient, it is highly selective about the information it takes in from all around. When you already hold a belief – in this case, that any request or suggestion that you change or behave a certain way puts your authentic self at risk – your confirmation bias is activated, seeking all the evidence it can find that the authentic you is not the right fit for where you are, and that if you want to be truly valued for who you are and to get ahead without compromising your authenticity, you need to go elsewhere.

3. You self-sabotage

You'll miss opportunities for personal growth and professional development which could not only bring professional rewards, but personal ones too. Nobody enjoys negative feedback! It feels like we're under attack and our survival instinct makes us quick to defend and deflect. But it takes feedback to know that you need to change and, in many cases, to tell us how. If you are ambitious enough to want career progression, you need to be resilient enough to handle feedback. Not everything that feels like a threat to your authenticity is a positive opportunity to develop, but some things will be.

4. You block your own resourcefulness

As with the Diversity Distraction and the Inclusion Illusion, you may be so busy defending your authenticity that you block your own resourcefulness. What matters here is your capacity to grow and adapt and evaluate the merits of what's being asked of you – all of which is in danger of being overlooked if your attention is focused on resisting what is being asked of you, and resenting the way things are.

5. You create the result you wanted to avoid

You'll be holding so tightly to one aspect of your identity (for example, a particular communication style) that you won't recognise that it's compromising something else about your personality (for example, being empathetic).

You can refuse any suggestion that you change and risk sacrificing your career for an improvised sense of identity. You could decide that every day you are an imposter in your workplace and betraying your true self. You could view the decision to keep showing up to work and leaving certain parts of you at the door as a way of hiding who you truly are. You are free to do any of these things. But which of these options will serve you?

A different option that is available to you is to see an authenticity threat as an opportunity to know yourself better and as an opportunity for growth. You can see it as the nudge you need to fully explore who you are or as the trigger to either update your sense of self, based on more recent achievements and experiences, or even to create a new one based on who you want to be. By choosing this option, what you once perceived as an authenticity threat becomes instead, an identity check point: Who am I being? What behaviours am I choosing? How do I want to grow?

How to sidestep the Authenticity Trap

The strategy for avoiding the Authenticity Trap is the same as that for dodging the Diversity Distraction and sidestepping the Inclusion Illusion – by first anticipating the trigger and then being more intentional in how you respond.

What triggers me?

Ask yourself: when I feel my identity is being threatened, what's going on? Is it a throwaway comment? Does it happen during a more formal feedback meeting? Does the trigger always relate to the same issue or piece of feedback or am I triggered by comments on a number of issues? If so, what are they? For example, perhaps you only receive comments about the way you dress. Or maybe they are not even comments. Maybe you just get the impression or feeling that others disapprove of your appearance, even if nothing is said. Or perhaps it's less direct – like positive comments or comparisons being made to your white peers who have a very different style or way of doing things. You may even feel that the culture of your whole organisation is at odds with how you see yourself. Your firm may have a particular reputation for being aggressive negotiators, for example, and because that's not you, your authenticity feels under threat every time you walk into a negotiation. These are your triggers – the circumstances which make you feel threatened and which, if you react to them without careful reflection, have the potential to throw you off track.

How do I normally react?

The second step is to notice your default reaction when a trigger event occurs.

As you know from Chapter 4 (Diversity Distraction) and Chapter 5 (The Inclusion Illusion) your default reaction is a chain of events that involves your automatic thoughts about a situation, and the emotions, actions and results these thoughts produce. When you understand that all of these are connected, you discover how it's your thoughts about the trigger that drives the feeling of being threatened.

You can see this at work in Sharon's case. Constantly thinking "No one values me for who I am" (her thought) and "They just want to turn me into one of them" (another thought) made her feel powerless, unappreciated and trapped (her emotions). At this stage, it was inevitable that Sharon would feel that the only course of action was to protect the authentic part of her she felt was under attack and try to escape, resulting in her missing not only the opportunity to develop professionally but also the potential for promotion in her current firm.

What thoughts go through your mind when you are triggered by an authenticity threat? Perhaps your thought is: "I can't be myself here" Or maybe your thought is "The only way to get promoted here is to compromise who I am." Once you have identified your typical thought pattern, you can work through the chain to see how your automatic reaction to an authenticity threat is keeping you trapped:

- How do these thoughts make me feel? (emotion)

- How am I showing up when I feel like this? (emotion)

- What am I doing/not doing as a result? (action)

- What results am I creating? (results)

How can I change my response?

The way to avoid the Authenticity Trap then is to change your response to it. You can do this by being more intentional about your thoughts when you're triggered, so that the resulting emotions you feel and action you then take create a better result.

I helped Sharon to do this using powerful coaching questions that challenged her beliefs about what it means to be authentic. This was not about convincing Sharon that her beliefs were wrong. It was about helping her to identify the areas where her fear of being inauthentic was getting in the way of her seeing an opportunity for growth; and to encourage her to review the integrity of other behaviours she had been pinning her identity to. As a result, Sharon gradually went from feeling threatened every time she received feedback to feeling much more empowered because she understood she had a choice about how to respond. This meant she was able to avoid the Authenticity Trap and learn from feedback that sup-

ported her growth, and make more conscious and confident decisions about the behaviour she was not willing to
change.

Below are examples of coaching questions you can use to
help you challenge your automatic response when something triggers an authenticity threat:

- How do I see myself?

- What does being authentic mean to me?

- How long have I been this way?

- How have I changed?

- How do I know when I'm being authentic?

- What am I pretending not to know?

- Where do I need to grow?

These questions will help you separate behaviour and
personality traits that are truly authentic from those that
you have unconsciously acquired over time. I know this
sounds a little daunting. But as you've seen, you have
more to lose from not doing this work than from doing it.
You could fall into the Authenticity Trap and end up stuck
fighting the wrong battle and never succeeding.

What does this bring up for you?

These questions may not sound like the secret to succeeding in a white world. You may even feel threatened by them! It's not unusual to want to resist the idea that you look at your own thoughts and reactions and adapt these in order to get a different result – particularly when it feels like those around you aren't doing enough to change their own thoughts and reactions. The way I approach this is the way I approach everything and that is to ask myself, which approach feels like giving my power away, and which one feels like I'm taking my power back?

Avoiding the Authenticity Trap requires a commitment to self-reflection and a willingness to challenge the way you see yourself and why. If you're thinking this all sounds great on paper but wondering where and how on earth to start, don't worry. In Part III, I'm going to give you a tool to help you do this work and then walk you through the process step by step so that by the end of this book you'll know exactly who you are and how to use that to help you succeed.

Summary

» As a person of colour striving to succeed in a white world, there will be times when you feel you can't be your authentic self.

» But beware the "Authenticity Trap" – the belief that you can't be authentic and get ahead.

» The battle to succeed in a world where the dominant culture differs from yours, is a battle you can win.

» Understand what triggers a threat to your authenticity.

» Challenge your thinking around these threats and what it means to be authentic.

» Be intentional in how you respond.

THE RACISM ROADBLOCK

*"I thrive on obstacles. If I'm told that it can't
be done, then I push harder."*

- ISSA RAE

As a high potential person of colour battling to succeed in a white world, you may have experienced or been subjected to racism in any number of guises. As we discussed in Part I, incidents of overt racism may be less frequent than they have been for past generations, but racism lives on in the many micro-aggressions sustained by people of colour every day. These micro-aggressions are hard to tolerate. The frustration of not being equally treated or valued doesn't go away. Without a strategy for dealing with racism, the injury grows and grows, compounding your Imposter Syndrome, until it feels like something insurmountable – a battle you just can't win.

But racism doesn't have to stop you. With the right tools, it's a battle you can win. To achieve this, we have to take a look at your thoughts about racism and your belief that racism is a barrier that must be lifted before you can succeed. The thought is: "I can't succeed until the circumstances around me change." I call this the Racism Roadblock because it takes away your power and blocks you from the path to success. This chapter is not about disputing the devastating impact of racism on the aspirations and opportunities of people of colour. It's about helping you find your power so that you can stay on track and be part of the solution. By the end of this chapter, you'll know how to spot when you're in danger of hitting the Racism Roadblock, and you'll have the awareness and the tools to help you sidestep it and take back your power. You'll discover that you can anticipate the Racism Roadblock and that when you have the tools to navigate your way around it, the battle to succeed in an often racist world is a battle you can win.

Let's be clear. Racism is a major issue and is something you should never have to tolerate. As we've seen from the surge in support of the Black Lives Matter movement, a vast number of your white colleagues and peers agree with this, and want to help to change this. But unfortunately, as a person of colour striving for success in a white world, it is something that you will encounter from time to time until the day when Martin Luther King's dream comes true and racism is forever eradicated. In the meantime, I'm going to show you how to respond to racism in an intentional way that will make it easier to create the results you want.

JENNY'S STORY

Jenny was born in the UK to a white English father and a Jamaican mother. She is smart, articulate and has a strong sense of purpose. One of the reasons for her approaching me was to enable her to find greater purpose in her work, or otherwise move to a role that afforded her this opportunity. In our career coaching sessions, it was apparent from the outset that before Jenny could get clear about her next career move, there was an issue that was presenting in her current position that was impacting upon her confidence and sense of how valued she felt.

One of these issues stemmed from a comment that had been made about Jenny being "a strong black woman" – not once, but on several occasions by different people. It was clear from the emotion in Jenny's voice and her choice of language that she perceived this as a racist slur. She felt that she was being tarnished by a racial stereotype that proved how little she was valued and understood. Not entirely understanding what was going on, I asked Jenny to explain. "Well, people think black women are stronger than other women, and that they have a higher pain threshold." I was fascinated. I had never heard this.

After spending time exploring the circumstances in which this came up for Jenny, I asked her a simple question: "is it true?"

Jenny paused to consider. Her eyes flicked up and stayed fixed at the upper left corner of her vision. I could almost see the machinations of her brain as they analysed and processed her thoughts, behaviours and approach. "Well, I have strong opinions, and I like to speak my mind. I'm not easily intimidated. Oh, and I've been through a lot to get here. Yes. I guess you could say I'm strong. And obviously, I'm black. And a woman. So yeah. I guess you could say I'm a strong black woman!"

Twenty minutes into our first coaching session and Jenny had already had a breakthrough. All this time, she had reacted to this comment as an insult; as something to denigrate and belittle her, that reflected how little she was valued by her colleagues. She had felt like the victim of a racial slur that would follow her around and block her progress. As a result of the work we did on this issue, Jenny was able to embrace her identity as a strong black woman in a positive way and step into the value and the power of that.

Jenny still hears comments like this and her old way of thinking wants to jump back to her old conclusions: if they valued me they wouldn't refer to me in that way. Why are they describing me like that? Why don't they say that about anyone else? Does this mean they don't value me?

But now she knows better. She knows that this line of thinking is just going to block her from the path to achieving her goal, which was to move up to the next level. She realises that although she is suspicious of the motives of those who refer to her that way, she was giving too much power away in focusing on what she felt they were or weren't trying to say. It was so much better and more empowering, she discovered, to focus on herself and find a way to make this an asset. And it's been amazing watching Jenny do this. Jenny discovered that if she started talking about herself in that way, it made her feel more in control. She could manage the messaging around "strong", so it aligns more with her personality and it seems, at least from her perspective, to shift the balance of power back into her control.

Does Jenny's experience resonate with you? Perhaps the people around you are always commenting on or (even worse!) touching your hair. Maybe some of your white colleagues always mispronounce your name or revert to racial stereotypes rather than get to know you. Or perhaps it's worse. Maybe you have had to endure working for a white boss who makes overtly racist comments in your presence and thinks that it's OK.

HOW TO SPOT THE RACISM ROADBLOCK

It can be hard to spot the Racism Roadblock because the thoughts and behaviours that define it feel so justified. How many of the following apply to you?

- The word "micro-aggressions" is a regular feature in your vocabulary.

- If someone commits a micro-aggression, you call them a racist.

- When you experience rejection, negative feedback or you see a white colleague succeeding ahead of you, you assume it's down to racism.

- You assume the racist act or comment of one partner or colleague is representative of the whole firm, company or institution.

- You let people mispronounce your name, and never correct them.

- You label the person or organisation, not the behaviour.

- You view explicit racism and implicit racism as equally offensive.

- You believe that anyone who isn't vocally "anti-racist", is racist.

How the Racism Roadblock keeps you stuck

When the racism is implicit or comes in the form of micro-aggressions like these, you feel disrespected and believe that your organisation will never value you enough to let you progress. When racism is more direct, it is belittling, insulting and offensive. The temptation, in either case, is to make it mean that you are in the wrong place and the only option available to you is to leave.

The problem with this type of *thinking* is that it takes away your power and gives it all to the perpetrator. In the short-term, the right solution might seem to be removing yourself from a situation in which you feel you are not valued or equal, but in the long-term, you are the one left with the derailed career. All you get to walk away with is

"

*When you
walk away from
racism, you walk
away from the
opportunity to
change it.*

"

a feeling of being cheated and wronged. The pattern of negative thinking to negative results follows the same pattern in relation to racism as we saw in previous chapters in relation to diversity, inclusion and authenticity. Each time you experience or witness an act of racism, the following happens:

1. You feel powerless, frustrated and resentful

When you see your chances of success as being entirely dependent on those around you recognising the error of their ways and changing their behaviour, you'll feel powerless. You have no direct control over what others think and how they behave. If there are people around you who – no matter how persuasive or right you may be – refuse to acknowledge that racism is a problem or refuse to work on themselves in order to change, you're left feeling frustrated and resentful – maybe even angry.

2. Your confirmation bias is activated

That clever, efficient brain of yours will get to work, scanning your environment and your relationships for evidence to support the racism in your organisation. It will completely ignore those of your colleagues or bosses who support you and value your contributions, preferring instead to focus only on the one obnoxious leader in your group who thinks he is somehow exempt from the responsibility of affording his employees of colour with the respect and recognition every human being deserves.

3. You self-sabotage

You'll be so busy feeling powerless, you won't notice or entertain the idea of there being opportunities which could help you progress your career. As a result, you'll miss opportunities to be part of the solution and re-educate others about their behaviour.

The other consequence of feeling you have no choice but to walk is the missed opportunity for growth – both for you and the perpetrator. For you, it's the opportunity to step into the power of both your identity and what makes you different, and then wear that difference as a source of pride. It's also an opportunity to educate the accidental racist – those whose racist acts are clothed in good intentions – around how to be better; and call out the intentional racist on behaviour that is totally unacceptable.

One of the most important developments to emerge as part of the Black Lives Matter protest, launched in response to the killing of George Floyd in Minneapolis earlier this year, was the outpouring of videos, articles and social media posts on what constitutes racism. Particularly fascinating to me was the number of my white friends and connections who confessed to realising for the first time, that they're "probably a bit racist" and had had no idea. They welcomed the opportunity to be better educated and demonstrate their commitment to getting it right. When you walk away from racism, you walk away from the opportunity to change it.

4. You block your own resourcefulness

If "those around me need to change" is the focus of all your attention, you forget the resources and skills available to you to influence that change: resilience, communication skills, the ability to influence, persuade and prove others wrong, and the ability to lead and inspire. With resources like these, you can go into battle and defy all manner of odds.

5. You create the result you wanted to avoid

You want to feel valued and be treated equally. However, by showing up from a position of powerlessness and resentment, overlooking opportunities and ignoring your own resources, you can end up compromising your own performance. This, in turn, may cause others to question your value and treat you differently to those who are showing up and performing well. In Jenny's case, her powerlessness and frustration caused her to become increasingly withdrawn. She felt less and less confident in her skin, making her question herself. The opposite scenario could also happen: you become increasingly vocal or confrontational in your refusal to tolerate such treatment. While understandable, neither of these reactions are helpful. There's a real danger they will backfire, creating an even greater barrier between you and those around you and a deeper experience of inequality.

It doesn't have to be that way. The racism you experience around you can trick you into thinking that we need racism to be fixed before we can succeed. In fact, racism is our motivation to succeed. When you change the way you respond to the racism that you encounter you hold onto your power in a way that helps you achieve success and become part of the solution.

How to sidestep the Racism Roadblock

The way you navigate the Racism Roadblock is by being intentional in your response to situations in which racism occurs. How you do this is the same way you changed your reaction to the lack of diversity around you and the lack of inclusion: you find the triggers, understand your automatic response and you choose a response that will help you stay on track.

What triggers me?

Ask yourself: when I feel someone is being racist towards me, what's going on? When does it occur and how often? Where does it normally take place? Is it one particular person who treats me this way, or is it a whole group? And if so, how many are we talking about? It's important to be really specific, because your brain will want to jump to the conclusion that your whole organisation is racist. If this is the case, it's going to be really hard to find a range of options beyond "I need to leave". For example, it could be that every time you have a conversation with a particular colleague, they make a comment about your hair. Or perhaps whenever you attend meetings there is someone (one person or perhaps everyone?) who assumes you are the most junior person in the room and that the white person beside you (who is significantly more junior than you) is in charge. Or maybe you find it offensive or racist when your organisation puts on a BAME event, clumping every non-white ethnicity into one amorphous group. These are your triggers – the circumstances which leave you feeling disrespected and undervalued and lead you to want to abandon all hope of succeeding where you are.

How do I normally react?

The second step to being intentional in your response is to understand your default reaction when a trigger event occurs.

Your default reaction is a chain of events that involves the automatic thoughts you have in response to a trigger, and the emotions, actions and results that follow from these thoughts. The secret to bypassing the Racism Roadblock is understanding this chain of events and being more intentional about where they lead.

Let's go back to Jenny. Jenny's thoughts that "All they see when they look at me is their idea of a black woman" and "they can't see past the colour of my skin" (her thoughts) made her feel powerless (emotion) which affected Jenny in two ways: first, she withdrew into herself and performed less well as a result; and secondly, the stress and anxiety of her experience with her current employer made her want to ensure that her next career move (the issue she came to me for help with) would be to the same or a lesser role in a lower-ranking company so that she wouldn't have to deal with such feelings going forward.

What thoughts go through your mind when you are triggered? Perhaps your thought is "what is wrong with these people?" Or maybe your thought is "this is not the place for me" or "I'm sick of being treated like I'm second class."

Once you have identified your typical thoughts, you can work through the chain of emotions, actions and results to see how your default reaction is going to block your success or help you stay on track:

- How do these thoughts make me feel? (emotion)

- How am I showing up when I feel like this? (emotion)

- What am I doing/not doing as a result? (action)

- What results am I creating? (results)

Honestly, I know it isn't easy to ask these questions of yourself! It can feel like you are being asked to take responsibility for the racism you're being subjected to. When your brain starts thinking this way, remember that this solution is not about everybody around you. It's about you and how you find your power in these challenging situations.

How can I change my response?

The way to bypass the racism around you so that it doesn't block your success and so you can take back your power is to change your thinking around it, so you can find a way to produce different results. You have a choice about how you respond to racism. Choose a response that serves you.

When someone mispronounces your name, there is a whole range of options open to you: for example, you could suppress your anger and walk away without saying a word, storing your anger and frustration up for when you get home so you can express it to your partner as evidence of how racist your workplace is; you could point out to the perpetrator that they are pronouncing your name wrong, show them how to pronounce it, and tell them that it's important to you that they get it right; you could write off the incident as yet another demonstration of how useless your experienced but otherwise out of touch boss is when it comes to communicating with members of his team.

When someone asks to touch your hair, again, you have a choice about what you make it mean and what you do. One of the many choices open to you in response to this and other acts of explicit and implicit racism is to call it out. But even within that choice, you have options. You can call it out in a way that is loaded with judgement and anger, or you can call it out in a way that educates the perpetrator and leaves space for rebuilding the relationship.

Nothing here is intended to suggest there is a right or wrong response to racism. The important message is that in a situation where it would be easy (and understandable) to feel powerless, you know you have more power than you think. That power comes from knowing there is always a choice and being intentional about the choice you make so that it is one that serves you.

You may be finding this challenging to accept or to put into practice. Here are some powerful coaching questions that I use with my clients:

- What am I assuming?

- What am I making it mean?

- Is this serving me, or will it throw me off track?

- What other options do I have?

- What can I learn from this?

- What can I teach?

- What's going on within me?

- Is it true?

Jenny, who we met earlier, made a breakthrough as a result of our coaching work together: she became more willing to share parts of her personal life with her colleagues. She realised that her defensiveness around who she was outside of work stemmed from her fear of how she would be judged and labelled. Gradually, as Jenny's confidence is growing, she is starting to see the benefits of opening up a little more: her colleagues have a much broader frame of reference for interacting with her and talking about her – a fact that became apparent when a white colleague introduced her to a friend who shared the same interest in ballroom dancing!

What does this bring up for you?

If you are struggling with this approach or feel sceptical about it, I do get it. The notion of racism as a roadblock, that it's up to you to transcend or fix, is not an easy one to sell. It's probably no coincidence that this chapter was one of the hardest chapters for me to write! The psychological effects of sustained racial abuse over time cannot be over-stated. But there's something even more debilitating and destructive than racism: that's the belief that you have no power against it.

But trust me, this approach is a game-changer. I've used this approach in my life and would not be where I am today were it not for my ability to see my choices and my determination not to relinquish my power to a system that would otherwise have held me down.

Now you know how to anticipate the Racism Roadblock, and you have the tools to navigate your way around it, you know that the battle to succeed in an often racist world is a battle you can win. It is also a tremendous opportunity for you to grow. What's required of you, if you are going to navigate this challenge as often as you encounter it, is exactly what will serve you as a leader going forward: the ability to have difficult conversations, to persuade and educate but also be willing to learn. It's going to take all your courage and resilience. You're going to need to feel sure of who you are and be able to stay in your power. You'll find the tools to help you do this in Part III.

Summary

» As a person of colour striving to succeed in a white world, you are going to encounter racism which could threaten your success.

» But beware the "Racism Roadblock" – the belief that racism needs to be eradicated before you can get ahead.

» The battle to succeed in a world where racism endures is a battle you can win.

» Understand what triggers you.

» Challenge your default reaction.

» Be intentional in how you respond.

PART III

THE BATTLE AGAINST
SELF-DOUBT

INTRODUCTION TO PART III

In Part I, we talked about the origins and impact of Imposter Syndrome and why, as a high potential person of colour striving to succeed in a white world, your experience of Imposter Syndrome is uniquely challenging.

In Part II, we talked about the battle you're fighting against systemic bias. I warned you about the Diversity Distraction, the Inclusion Illusion, the Authenticity Trap and the Racism Roadblock and gave you the tools to navigate your way around them so you can triumph over bias and stay on track.

In Part III, we're turning our attention to the internal battle you're fighting against Imposter Syndrome. We are going to look at your thoughts about who you are, and examine how those thoughts are getting in your way.

If you have been battling with systemic bias, you may not have been paying much attention to how your thoughts about yourself have been holding you back. You think that if systemic bias went away and there was better equality in your workplace, then you'd have a clear pathway to success. But the systemic bias around you is an aggravating factor to your Imposter Syndrome. It is not the root cause. Systemic bias isn't responsible for your Imposter Syndrome. You are.

You'll discover that Imposter Syndrome is the result of thoughts you have about yourself and what you are making these thoughts mean. Until now you've believed that your Imposter Syndrome was a weakness that was holding you back, and that you needed to conquer, overcome or ditch it before you could succeed. In Part III, I'm going to show you that the opposite is true. Your Imposter Syndrome isn't a weakness. It's a strength. If you want to succeed and to fulfil your potential, the answer isn't to resist it, it's to embrace it and then use it as a source of strength.

To help you achieve this, I'm going to introduce you to a powerful tool for investigating, understanding and accepting who you are. As a result of doing the work in this section, you'll have a deeper understanding of the role that Imposter Syndrome is playing in your life and how it is, in fact, the source of your power and the key to why you are so uniquely valuable. This understanding will leave you feeling more confident and empowered, and motivate you to go out into the world and fulfil more of your potential.

REFRAMING
IMPOSTER SYNDROME

"If you surrender to the wind,
you can ride it."

- TONI MORRISON

n this chapter, we're going to look at some of the solutions to Imposter Syndrome you may have tried in the past, and why they haven't worked. You'll discover that it's not your Imposter Syndrome that is holding you back, it's your resistance to it. But the time for resistance has passed. It's time for a new approach.

By the end of this chapter, you're going to see your Imposter Syndrome in a completely different light. I'm going to show you how to accept your Imposter Syndrome and embrace it as a part of who you are, so that it can become a source of strength.

Solutions that sometimes work

Google "How to overcome Imposter Syndrome" and you'll be inundated with answers. The solutions range from telling you what to tell yourself ("tell yourself you can do it") and telling you how to treat yourself ("be kind to yourself") to even changing how your brain works ("rewrite your mental programmes"). You'll find solutions that target your fear of failure ("reframe failure as a learning opportunity", "don't focus on your failures") and others that target your success ("own your successes!", "visualise success!"). Some solutions call for a challenge ("challenge negative thoughts") while others advise a simple acknowledgement ("acknowledge your feelings"). There are solutions based upon logical evaluation ("consider the context", "understand your strengths and weaknesses") and solutions that recommend enlisting the support of others ("call a friend", "seek support" or "talk to others"). If your goal is to get rid of Imposter Syndrome, there is no shortage of strategies for you to try.

How many of these solutions sound familiar? Which have you tried and how effective did you find them? Perhaps one or more of these have worked for you in the past. In my talks on Imposter Syndrome, I like to encourage a discussion around the many solutions that are out there, the strategies people are trying and how well these strategies are working, if your goal is to get rid of your Imposter Syndrome. What this discussion always reveals is that some of these solutions work some of the time; and some solutions work for some people and not for others. But is that enough?

For me, the answer is no, and there are three reasons why they aren't enough for you either:

A unique problem can't be solved with an everyday solution

The first is that Imposter Syndrome is no ordinary form of self-doubt that can be held at bay with a few well-meaning words – not from yourself, your best friend, a trusted boss; not even your mum. In Chapter 1, we examined the qualities that make it unique: the fact that the more you succeed, the worse it can get; that it has no grounding in reality (the fact that you have achieved all of this success is, frankly, irrelevant) and that it's hidden. Because of this, tips and tricks that tell you what to do in the moment are all very well, but their impact is limited. If they work at all, the effect is temporary. Your Imposter Syndrome will come right back again. This may be fine if your form of Imposter Syndrome is mild and occasional, but if your Imposter Syndrome is deep-rooted and ongoing, these solutions simply aren't enough.

Nothing changes

The second reason these solutions are inadequate is that they don't actually *change* anything. You may be able to use these strategies to get you past the hurdle now in front of you, but as soon as you encounter another challenge or you step out of your comfort zone again, you're back to square one. The panic rises, the anxiety returns and you're left scrambling around wondering why the solution that worked for you last time doesn't work anymore. Or, if you'd been under the illusion that your Imposter Syndrome was cured, you'll be feeling frustrated and anxious about its return.

KIM'S STORY

When I first started coaching Kim, she had just been promoted to partner in a large UK law firm. I remember being surprised when she told me, during our very first session, that she used to have Imposter Syndrome, but that it was no longer an issue. But less than one month later, as Kim told me during her second session, her Imposter Syndrome was back. Her frustration and disappointment were evident. "I thought I'd got rid of it," she said, "but it's back!" When I asked what solutions had worked before, she told me it was by repeatedly telling herself that she had worked hard to get where she was. Repeating this message to herself had worked for her in the short-term, but in the long-term nothing had changed. As soon as she was promoted and found herself once again out of her comfort zone, her Imposter Syndrome came flooding back.

Solutions like those listed above only treat the symptoms. Feeling like a fraud, thinking you don't deserve your success, perfectionism, the fear of exposure, an inability to internalise your success – these are all *symptoms* of Imposter Syndrome. They are not the cause. As we saw in Chapter 1, the cause is rooted in how you experience what makes you different to those around you, and what you are making that mean about who you are and your chances of success.

Not powerful enough

The third reason solutions like this are not enough for a high potential person of colour like you striving to succeed in a white world and for whom awareness of this difference is all the more evident, felt and pronounced, is that these tactics simply aren't powerful enough in the face of systemic bias that penalises you for that difference. Trying to solve your Imposter Syndrome with tools like "tell yourself you can do it" and "acknowledge your feelings" is like trying to cut through concrete with a spoon. The tool just isn't up to the task. What you need is something more powerful. Something that is going to create a seismic shift in the balance of power between you and the obstacles and challenges in front of you.

The bigger the battle you are facing against self-doubt, the further and deeper your solution needs to go. And because you are fighting two battles, you need a solution that goes *all the way*. This doesn't just come from my clients' experiences. It comes from my own.

MY IMPOSTER AWAKENING

On a grey rainy day in June 2015, I found myself standing outside Waterstones bookshop in Piccadilly, London, bursting with excitement. Waterstones Piccadilly is no ordinary bookshop. It is five floors of a booklover's paradise. It's a place I rarely find the time to visit and when I do find time, it's a quick hit and run book purchase squeezed into a busy workday. However, the day in question was no ordinary day. It was the day I had been promising myself for months: I had given myself permission to spend a whole morning just looking at books – browsing covers and book titles in search of inspiration for the cover of my newly completed first book. I had finally finished the man-uscript and sent it off to the editor the day before.

But just five minutes into this treat of an experience, I started to panic. My heart started pounding in my chest and my palms began to sweat. And then there it was – the all too familiar voice in my head saying: "Caroline, what are you doing here? Publishing a book? Who do you think you are? You're a fraud. And if you do this, everyone will know. You'll be exposed and you'll lose everything." A wave of nausea washed over me. I felt an uncontrollable urge to run.

Anxious, I left Waterstones in a hurry and made my way home as quickly as I could. I desperately needed to hide. Once home, I locked myself away in the makeshift office attached to the side of my house where the heating doesn't work and the lights seem to short circuit every five minutes. It felt like an appropriate set up for curling up into a ball and wallowing in the realisation that, after all I'd achieved and everything I'd been through, I still felt like a fraud. When I left my legal career ten years previously, following the birth of my second son, Noah, I was so sure I had left my Imposter Syndrome behind. I was wrong.

Not only have I experienced this for myself, I've seen it happen with others many times – Imposter Syndrome sufferers who change careers or employers, thinking their Imposter Syndrome will go away. But everywhere you go, there you are. As I learned from personal experience, your Imposter Syndrome isn't something outside of you that you can leave behind, it's within you.

Believe me, I'd tried. You know the solutions we've already talked about – the ones you may have discovered and tried for yourself – I tried them too. I've tried and tested them for years, hoping they would help. But all they seemed to offer me was the pretence that I wasn't an imposter, when I felt everything about my life and journey to this point screamed that I was. I was a woman of colour who had been striving to succeed in a white world my whole life. I didn't just feel like an imposter as a black woman walking around a bookshop full of books written by white people, I was an imposter.

On that unforgettable day in June, I realised my mistake. All this time I'd been searching for a way to fix my Imposter Syndrome. But my Imposter Syndrome didn't feel like something I could "overcome" or "conquer" or "ditch". It felt like a part of me. So, after trying all the other solutions I'd used with only limited success in the past, I decided to try the one solution I hadn't yet tried: instead of trying to fight it, I decided to accept it.

Accepting it meant turning to face Imposter Syndrome to see it for what it was. The moment I did this, I saw the truth: I felt like an imposter because I was one.

Something in me shifted. I realised that Imposter Syndrome wasn't a menacing monster sent to terrorise me. It was like an old friend. After all, it had been there through every step of my journey. Every time I'd faced a challenge or setback, it was as if my Imposter Syndrome had been pushing me to think about who I was and where I was, and reminding me why I was there and the journey I'd taken to get there.

I started to consider all the different roles Imposter Syndrome had played in my life until that point. It was the courage I'd shown when I was afraid of failure but still took that next step; it was all the successes I'd achieved, even if I had been too blind to recognise or internalise them at the time; it was the ambition that pushed me to be the best, and made me strive for success even in a white world where systemic bias would try to hold me down; it was the reason I was here (wherever here was at the time), facing yet another challenge, another battle that I feared I couldn't win. It was every one of my failures, my darkest moments and the times I had picked myself up, dusted myself off, licked my wounds and kept going. My Imposter Syndrome was me.

Acceptance

If you're a person of colour striving to succeed in a white world, you are an imposter. You can try to resist, but when you consider all the ways you are different you'll realise that this is about the truth of it.

As a person of colour who has reached your level of success in a white world, I know you're used to fighting. You've had to fight a war on two fronts to get to where you are today. So I understand that embracing your Imposter Syndrome and accepting that you are an imposter may feel like a monumental task. But the minute you stop resisting, you'll see things from a whole new perspective and a dramatic shift will begin to take place. Your circumstances won't change, but how you experience them, and what you are able to do with them will. Situations and people that previously put you down won't be able to hold you back any more. As you've seen from my story in Chapter 3, statistics, names, stereotypes, setbacks, being excluded, prejudice – none of these can stop you. When you accept, understand and welcome what makes you different, everything changes.

The benefits of acceptance

Acceptance is easily misunderstood. You may think it's a resignation, a surrender from a point of weakness, but the opposite is true. When you accept something, you gain authority over it. Because you're no longer resisting and fighting with the way things are, you can see things more clearly, and see options that weren't previously available to you. But it takes courage. Accepting I am an imposter took courage because it meant facing the truth of all the reasons I was different to those around me – reasons that related to my ethnicity, my socio-economic background, my childhood, and how my struggle for success differed from my white peers and colleagues.

What does accepting you are an imposter mean for you? What difference does it magnify? For sure, your ethnicity. What else? As a reward for having the courage to accept this, like me you'll gain a whole new perspective on the role Imposter Syndrome has played in your life to date and on what those imposter feelings and fears will mean for you going forward. You'll discover that your Imposter Syndrome isn't something you need to fix. It is the expression of what makes you unique and valuable, and therefore something you need to hold onto. When you understand this, you realise that nothing about your Imposter Syndrome says weakness. Everything about it says strength. When you choose acceptance, here's what you learn:

> *Acceptance taught me that life is an arena designed to challenge you.*

Lesson 1: Your Imposter Syndrome is here to stay

Why is Imposter Syndrome so prevalent? Why are there so many solutions and suggestions for curing it, conquering it, and yet so few people who are cured? Have you ever wondered why your Imposter Syndrome is so deep-seated and why you feel it's something you'll never escape? Acceptance taught me that the reason for this is because Imposter Syndrome is part of my identity and it's here to stay. That discovery freed me from the tyranny of feeling like a victim and created space for me to stop fighting who I thought I was and take a proper, closer look at the truth.

If you're finding this concept hard to accept, you're not the only one. I know that when people show up to my talks they are looking for concrete answers. By far the most popular reason for attending is to find out how to make Imposter Syndrome go away. The last thing they want to hear, and perhaps the last thing you were expecting to read in this book, is that your Imposter Syndrome is here to stay, and that the solution is not to fix it, it's to embrace it.

Lesson 2: Life is an arena

Why is there always a challenge ahead? Why are the circumstances around you or the conditions you find yourself in rarely easy? I've certainly wondered that a few times in the past! But it's not only you and me; why do so many of us have battles to fight and difficult life experiences to navigate?

Acceptance taught me that life isn't a playground designed to entertain you and where your sole purpose is to have fun and play safely. Acceptance taught me that life is an arena designed to challenge you. It's the place where your sole purpose is to grow and take risks so you can fulfil your potential.

Lesson 3: You are in the right place

Why are your most challenging experiences so often the most rewarding in retrospect? Why is it, that when you look back on a failure, difficulty or setbacks, you so often think it was the best thing that could have happened? Or if not the best thing, then the thing that taught you something you really needed to learn? You can never see it in the moment when you're in the thick of it, but you see it when you're looking back.

Acceptance taught me that there's a reason for the challenges in front of me. It taught me this was exactly where I was supposed to be because of what I needed to learn for the next stage of my growth.

Lesson 4: You are a gladiator

Have you ever wondered why, when you're watching a movie or witnessing a battle or struggle play out in real life, you always side with the underdog? Why did you want David to beat Goliath? Why did we all cheer when Japan beat South Africa in the quarter-finals of the 2020 Rugby World Cup (I have a house full of rugby players, there was no escaping it!)? Why is *Slumdog Millionaire* such an incredible story (if you haven't seen it, the clue is in the title)? Why is the most frequently watched family movie in my house *Cool Runnings* – the movie about the Jamaican bobsleigh team who entered the 1988 Winter Olympics in Canada, and one of the best underdog stories of all time (please tell me you've seen it)? Why do I love Denzel Washington in *Man of Fire*; Michael B. Jordan in *Creed*? Why do we never want those with all the power and the biggest advantage to win? Have you considered why, even if the underdog loses, you still feel happy because you saw how hard they fought, how courageous they were, how their determination and passion and hard work took them way beyond where it was possible or believable for them to go?

The act of acceptance leaves no room for you to act the victim or play small. It emboldens you to step up to the challenge of fulfilling your potential, even when it's hard. Acceptance teaches us that to be an imposter is to be the underdog in the story, the gladiator in life's arena. You might be offended, ignored and devalued; you may be excluded and prejudged. Most certainly there will be moments when you will feel isolated and alone, when you will think to yourself, "What's the point when it's this hard?" and you will want to give up. Acceptance doesn't make any of this OK, but it does give you power and authority over Imposter Syndrome in situations where you might otherwise feel you have no control. You get to step into the arena and fight battles you think you can't win, knowing that the way to win is the way that gladiators win: in the way you show up, and keep showing up – by going all-in with courage and determination; with passion and purpose.

This new understanding gave me a glimpse of what true confidence feels like, and I've been building on that confidence ever since. This was so much more powerful than telling myself to "own my successes" or "consider the context" or "admit that perfection isn't possible". It touched me at a much deeper level. Not only was the world different. I was different.

This is the transformation I want for you and your Imposter Syndrome. Now that you've started to see your Imposter Syndrome differently, you are ready to start using it to your advantage. In the next chapter, I'm going to give you a powerful tool to help you do that.

Summary

» Imposter Syndrome is a unique form of self-doubt that can't be solved with simple tips and tricks.

» The time for fighting your Imposter Syndrome has passed. It's time to try acceptance.

» You feel like an imposter because you are one.

» When you accept you're an imposter, your whole perspective changes.

» Nothing about your Imposter Syndrome spells weakness. It spells strength.

» Your Imposter Syndrome is here to stay.

» Life is an arena (not a playground).

» You're in the right place.

» You are a gladiator.

THE IMPOSTER SPEECH

"Identity is a prison you can never escape, but the way to redeem your past is not to run from it, but to try to understand it, and use it as a foundation to grow."

- JAY-Z

In this chapter, I introduce you to my Imposter Speech, a powerful tool that I created to transform your Imposter Syndrome into instant courage and lasting confidence. You'll learn what it is and where it comes from, how it works and how you can use it to take ownership of your Imposter Syndrome and win the battle against self-doubt.

This chapter will prepare you for the work you'll do in the coming chapters to create your own Imposter Speech. I'll explain the 5-step process you need to go through to create it so you know what to expect and can get excited about creating your own.

What is the Imposter Speech?

The Imposter Speech is an empowering personal statement that uses your Imposter Syndrome to build a powerful new identity, and pushes you to confidently show up as who you are. Most people with Imposter Syndrome show up to a challenge focussing on what they think they can't do, and then fear takes over. But when you use the Imposter Speech, you bring everything you are to the challenge. As a result, you become the main event and the fear of failure takes a back seat. This gives you access to the pool of knowledge, resources, qualities and experience you've been accumulating your whole life, so you get to show up as your most powerful self.

It's not an elevator pitch

The easiest way to describe the Imposter Speech is by starting with what is commonly known as the elevator pitch or elevator speech – itself a kind of power statement that reflects the image of yourself you'd like to project to the world. Originating in the 1970s, the idea behind it was that should you one day find yourself in an elevator (or lift, as we Brits prefer to say – although "lift pitch" doesn't have quite the same effect) and the CEO or senior partner walks in, what you say in the 30 seconds that follow could change your life. So you'd better be prepared for it! Crafting your value into a short punchy speech that is easy to

222

remember and can be pulled out at a moment's notice is the only way to ensure that you'll be prepared when an opportunity like that presents itself, or any other time you may need to project an impressive image of yourself. But while they are both personal statements, and both (once you have taken the time to learn them), are easily accessible and can be pulled out at a moment's notice, they are not the same thing. There's a distinction between the two and it's an important one.

It's for your eyes only

As with the elevator pitch, the Imposter Speech is a well-crafted speech that is short and punchy enough to be easy to remember and pull out at a moment's notice. But there's a fundamental difference that sets the Imposter Speech apart: it's not for your CEO or senior partner, or anyone else you may need or want to impress. It's for you. And only you. The reason for this is the need for absolute truth, a truth that can only be arrived at where there is no agenda. When you create a speech to impress others, you emphasise the good bits and do your best to exclude the rest. I mentioned above that the speech is structured around five questions which get to the core of who you are. Your answers to those questions form the backbone of the Imposter Speech and need to be authentic and honest. It's the truth of those answers that make the Imposter Speech such a powerful source of confidence.

When there is truth, the need to feel like a fraud, or hide away or pretend to be someone you're not falls away. The only way to get to this level of honesty is to make it for your eyes only.

Origins of the Imposter Speech

I've always loved reading. As a child, I only ever read fiction and, as with all great stories, there was always a heroine or a hero who battled impossible odds and somehow managed to succeed. Reading was my lifeline, my escape from the chaos and instability of growing up poor and black in a deprived and disadvantaged community. I loved those books.

Then one day, I was about 13 at the time, I stumbled upon a book called *The Power of Positive Thinking* by Norman Vincent Peale. It was the first non-fiction book I'd ever read and, although I didn't know it at the time, that book was my first introduction to some of the principles I now teach as a coach. Until that moment, I thought the world inside me was the place to go when I needed to escape. But after reading that book I discovered that the world inside of me was also the place to go when I needed to find my strength. I discovered that even though I had no control over what was going on in the world around me, I did have control over how I reacted to that world. I discovered that if I took control of my thinking, I would have control over

"

It's not what happens around you that decides your fate. It's how you think about it, and what you choose to do with it.

"

what happened next. For someone who had previously felt so powerless in relation to my circumstances, this was something I was incredibly excited to hear. The idea that I could think my way to a better outcome for myself totally blew my mind. From that moment on, I devoured more and more books with that same message: it's not what happens around you that decides your fate. It's how you think about it, and what you choose to do with it.

REVELATION IN A BOX

It's 1988, and suddenly and abruptly my newly adopted perspective on life meets its biggest test. I'm at Cranbrook School – the same school that I'd received the rejection letter from two years earlier – a grammar school in Kent where, through a combination of my mum's hustling and the generosity of strangers, I was lucky enough to board. I'm once again the only black student in the school but it doesn't matter, I love everything about it and more than anything, I love the friendships I have formed (which are my most treasured friendships to this day).

Mornings are a big deal at boarding school. That's when the post arrives, and when it does we are all giddy with excitement. "Who has a letter?" "Who is that huge parcel for?" "I can't believe you have another letter! You had one yesterday. And the day before!" and "Can I help you open it?"

This is 1988 when people still write letters in real hand-writing and send parcels bursting with goodies and gifts and opening those packages is the highlight of the day. It doesn't matter that the letters or parcels are almost never for me. It isn't really the point. When one girl receives a box of treats in the post, it is as if we all do.

On the day in question, I rush to the hall table like every-one else, to see how many letters have arrived and who they're for. On the table is a large parcel wrapped in brown parcel paper. The parcel is addressed to me.

You can imagine the excitement. Remember, I hardly ever get letters. I almost never get parcels. I couldn't believe it. Neither could anyone else. It was the most exciting moment. Ever.

I rush upstairs followed by a crowd of friends who all pile on to my bed to watch me open it, excited as I am to see the parcel's contents; eager and ready to catch the stray treats that will inevitably come tumbling out. I hold the box in my hand in disbelief and turn it over a few times, savouring the sheer joy of that moment, which meant that someone had been thinking of me. And then, unable to wait any longer, I tear the parcel open and lift the lid off the box and pull out a brown envelope with a logo stamp in bold black letters:

HM Prison Service.

I freeze. The blood drains from my face. The squealing and excitement stop and there is silence all around me. I open the envelope and read the letter.

Dear Caroline,

Your mother is no longer in our custody and we have no forwarding address, so we are returning all your letters.

The box slips from my hands and its contents cascade to the ground. Not the sweets and candy and little gifts we'd all been expecting. Just letters. What seems like hundreds of them. All of them with my home address written by the same careful hand; my hand. And all addressed to the same person: "Mum".

A cloud of shame envelops me and I can't even breathe. I feel a tsunami of pain and I can almost hear the explosion as the earth shatters beneath me. I am devastated.

Who am I? Where am I? What am I doing here?

My mum? In prison? All this time? The missed parents' evenings, the no shows on sports days and speech days – not because she was working but because she was in prison. The endless hours and countless occasions I waited in vain. The countless no-shows at bus shelters and railways stations where we'd arranged to meet, after hours of waiting – two hours, three hours, four hours and more – and searching the crowds for a familiar face. The unexplained disappearances, the confusion and the fear that clouded every encounter. And the letters. Those heartfelt letters I'd written week after week for months and then years. Until that day, I had justified every one of those disappointments blindly, eternally hopeful and trusting. I'd swallowed the pain of every abandonment and I'd been bravely holding on. But not that day.

I'd suffered from Imposter Syndrome years before that day, but this took things to a new low. I felt myself falling into a black hole, with only the vaguest awareness that everyone around me had slipped quietly away. I would have continued to fall, but my instinct for survival made me reach out. I grabbed the only thing left that made sense: it's not what happens around you that decides, it's what's going on inside of you.

Years later, at the time of my Waterstones crisis, when I finally decided to confront my Imposter Syndrome, my brain took me to the revelation in a box, the emotional earthquake that it caused and the questions that helped me find my power: Who am I? Where am I? What am I doing here?

I hadn't realised it, but the solution to my Imposter Syndrome had been with me the whole time.

Creating the Imposter Speech

The effect of the questions I'd asked myself as a teenager turned out to be every bit as potent when I was an adult and I went looking for the answers. I discovered that the person I felt myself to be in the moments when life was challenging and I felt most fearful was just the surface layer of who I was. Beneath that surface lay a lifetime of knowledge, experience, resources and aspirations, compacted over time into a core strength that was far more powerful than anything I could have imagined. The reason it had taken me so long to find it was because I hadn't known where to look.

Who am I? Where am I? Why am I here? These were the questions that told me where to start. How did I get here? Where am I going? These questions urged me to keep looking and emboldened me. The answers they produced gave me the courage and made me strong. The fear was still there. But my situation was starting to feel less of a threat, and more like an opportunity. The answers didn't just make me feel brave enough to take the next step. I felt excited about it.

Once I'd experienced the powerful effect of those questions, I was desperate to hold onto it. How could I hold onto this new idea of myself as being powerful, not in spite of everything I was but because of who I was? The next time my Imposter Syndrome came back, how could I access that courage and strength? How could I produce that excitement in the moments when I needed it most? I needed a tool I could carry around with me at all times and take out in any moment. Something that wouldn't be left behind when I changed my handbag or decided to wear a different coat. Not something that I had to carry on me (and therefore was in danger of forgetting). It needed to be in me. The answer was clear. I needed a speech.

I didn't really create the Imposter Speech, it created itself. In the end, it took no effort to mould those questions into a structured framework that I could carry around and draw on any time I needed it; which was easy to do when I felt compelled to share the power of the Imposter Speech with other Imposter Syndrome sufferers. It's almost as if the speech had always been there while I battled away on centre stage, waiting patiently in the wings until the moment it would finally dawn on me that I didn't need to wait for change out there. I had all the power I needed right here.

Who are you?

Where are you?

Why are you here?

How did you get here?

Where are you going?

When I formed the Imposter Speech in 2015, I was so excited to share it with my clients and audiences. I'll never forget the first time I shared the Imposter Speech tool with an audience at a leadership event for high potential people of colour at one of my corporate client organisations. The following morning I received an email from the organiser asking me what I had done. "People were visibly changed by your event," he told me. I've been humbled by its effect ever since. The Imposter Speech has helped me win battles I thought I could never win. It has helped clients in my workshops and on my programmes to find the power to win their battles, and now it's going to help you find yours.

How does the Imposter Speech work?

The Imposter Speech works by taking the life experiences and personal qualities that make you so unique and are at the heart of your Imposter Syndrome, and then moulding these into a powerful speech that connects you to all of your forgotten power. This is the power that's been hiding in your past successes, your core values, your past failures and your overall purpose. This power has been there all along, but until now either you haven't known it, or you've been unable to access it. The beauty of the Imposter Speech is that it converts that power into something practical, portable and usable.

It gives you instant courage

Because it's a speech that you can learn, the power your Imposter Speech releases can be accessed by you at any time. You can mutter it under your breath, say it out loud in the mirror or say it while walking down the street. As long as you keep using it, it will be there whenever you need it, ready to give you an instant boost of courage. I talk about specific scenarios for using your speech in more detail in Chapter 15.

It creates lasting confidence

But there's more. The speech also works as a building block for creating lasting confidence. Because you're using your speech each time you have imposter feelings, you begin to associate these feelings with more positive experiences. Over time, the thoughts "I'm a fraud" and "I don't deserve my success" become a trigger for you to step into your power and show up as the full extent of who you are. Over time, you begin to internalise the message that you are unique and extremely capable, and that you have all the resources you need to step up to the challenge in front of you. You don't just feel more confident. You become more confident.

It pushes you out of your comfort zone

One of the first changes I noticed from using my Imposter Speech was that I started to go all in. I made myself more visible, and I started setting more ambitious goals that I began to share more openly. I was all over social media talking about what I do, my value and how you could work with me. If you've seen me all over LinkedIn in recent years, this is the reason why!

It changes how you show up

It isn't easy winning clients, especially when you start a new business. If you are an employee, the equivalent for you would be building a business case, attracting clients or supporting your case for a promotion to continue to progress your career. Before I had my Imposter Speech I waited for success to come to me and to show me my worth and value. I played safe and concentrated on being diligent and not making any mistakes. I thought that if I did that, it would be enough and that the universe would reward me and show me results. It's amazing how many of you are taking the same approach to how you show up at work. But this passive approach to showing your value just isn't enough. You'll make some progress, but playing small produces small results.

Thanks to my Imposter Speech, I lost the victim mentality of being the only one in the room and stopped trying not to stand out. I did the opposite. I decided to be the first. My newly discovered power impacted everything: how I interacted at networking events, how I introduced myself, the goals I set, even the opportunities I saw – I saw them everywhere! It changed how I approached challenges and dealt with setbacks – I wasn't interested in distractions, traps or illusions. I was in the arena and I was showing up with everything I had.

I could go on. I could use this space to list how my client-base changed, or how many new clients I was able to win; I could name-drop the calibre of my clients and the impressive high-achieving individuals I have had the pleasure of working with since I stepped up my game. But if I do this you'll think it's all about the end result and you'll miss the greatest result to come out of your Imposter Speech and the real value it offers you: a deep-rooted confidence in who you are at your core, and your power to win battles you think you can't win.

Benefits of your Imposter Speech

Before we look at how the Imposter Speech works, let's talk about the benefits, so you can see why this solution goes so much further than any of the other solutions you've tried:

1. It builds your **confidence**, layer by layer, so it affects you at a much deeper level and can create a lasting transformation in the way you view yourself.

2. It is **authentic** and true. The only way to create your Imposter Speech is through a willingness to look deep inside and see what's really there.

3. It gives you **instant courage, motivation and resilience** when you need it. It works as a pep talk in the very moment when you need those resources. I give examples of how you can use it for this purpose in Chapter 15.

4. It's **for you**. It's a mirror talk, not an elevator pitch. It's not created for anyone else except you. So there's no confusion around trying to impress or sell yourself in your best light. Your Imposter Speech is 100% you, warts and all!

5. It's **adaptable**. You can use parts of the speech or all of the speech, depending on the circumstances

and what you want it to do. You can also create different versions of the speech to suit different scenarios.

6. It's **unique** to you. There's no one size fits all. Your Imposter Speech is tailor-made, so yours is the perfect fit for you.

7. **How you see yourself will change**. As you get better at internalising its message, you will see yourself as more valuable and, as a result, convey that value more effectively to others, who will start to see you that way too.

8. It is **future-proof.** Your speech is designed to evolve and grow as you do, and gain more experiences to draw from.

"I had no idea that being your authentic self could make me as rich as I've become. If I had, I'd have done it a lot earlier."

– OPRAH WINFREY

Creating your Imposter Speech

Over the next five chapters, you are going to create your Imposter Speech. Each chapter is dedicated to one step in the process. I'm going to show you how to mine the raw materials of your life experience for qualities that give you back your power, which you can then use in your life going forward in your battle for success. There are two parts to each step:

1. The process – which is the exploratory part of looking at where you are now and what may be standing in your way.

2. The speech – the short statement or sentences that syntheses what you have revealed in the process stage.

RULES FOR CREATING A POWERFUL IMPOSTER SPEECH

- You have to complete all 5 steps.

- No one can create it for you.

- You have to complete the process before answering the question.

- Don't think of others, think only of yourself.

- Be open and honest.

- Be brave and courageous.

- Don't expect to get it perfect first time, or ever. It's a work in progress.

- Ask for help if you need to.[12]

Don't expect to build a powerful speech in one sitting. You can rush through the 5-steps in a day and come out with a speech, but remember this speech is not a tip or trick. It's not a quick hack. It's a powerful tool that has the potential to be utterly transformational for you. To ensure you experience these results, I recommend you dedicate at least a week to each of the 5 steps, and a further week to bring all the elements of your speech together and start internalising it. If you're the sort of person who is motivated enough to do this sort of internal work on your own, I have created a free downloadable resource to help you work through the 5 steps. To access this, head over to **carolineflanagan.com/imposterspeech**. Why not head on over there now, so you have everything you need to get started?

Alternatively, if you want to add some accountability and inspiration, you can sign up to the Imposter Speech programme and do this process as part of a group (check out **carolineflanagan.com/imposterspeech/join** for more details) or attend an Imposter Speech workshop. I usually announce details of upcoming workshops via social media, so do make sure you connect with me on social media (you'll find details of how to connect with me at the back of this book).

The Imposter Speech works

The Imposter Speech works. If you follow the process in this book you'll experience a transformation in how you view yourself and what you can achieve as a person of colour in a white world. I've seen that transformation in my clients. I've experienced it myself. Now it's your turn.

You're about to change your life. Are you ready?

Let's create your speech.

CHAPTER 10

———————

WHO AM I?

*"We are constantly invited to
be who we are."*

- HENRY DAVID THOREAU

In Chapter 9, I introduced the Imposter Speech as a powerful tool to help you win the battle against self-doubt and systemic bias. As we've seen in the previous chapter, it does this by giving you courage in the exact moment that you need it, building layer upon layer of confidence internally over time. In this and subsequent chapters, I'm going to take you through the five-step process that will lead to your Imposter Speech – one step for each chapter. Each step is built around a single question you'll need to answer in order to create your Imposter Speech.

What is the first step of the Imposter Speech?

The first step of the Imposter Speech is the question: *"Who am I?"* The answer to the question, *"Who am I?"*

is an easy one – you simply state your name. But don't be fooled by its simplicity. This step is an important primer for the steps to come. Stating your name is the first piece in the puzzle of your new imposter identity which, when complete, is going to provide the powerful foundation that will support you going forward.

At the end of this chapter, you'll create a short statement about who you are to form the first line of your Imposter Speech, and I'm going to encourage you to start using this statement intentionally in your daily life.

The purpose of this step is to show you how valuable and important your name is and how it can be used as a powerful source of confidence. As a result of completing the work in this chapter, you will see your name in a new light. You'll feel more proud of it and connected to it, and you'll start to feel different when you say it. Eventually, it will become your most powerful confidence aid.

How knowing who you are helps with your Imposter Syndrome

A feature of Imposter Syndrome is the focus on who you are not. We constantly compare ourselves to our peers and others around us. We also project onto them all the qualities we feel we are lacking in ourselves and, in our minds, we make them more deserving or entitled than we are. Even if you have the same qualifications as your white peers and underwent the same rigorous selection process as they did, you still remain, as a high potential person of colour, permanently conscious of who you are not: a white person for whom surviving in a white world is easy.

Asking "Who am I?" is the first step in switching your focus back to where it belongs: to you. We want to break the negative cycle of you feeling less than, or not enough, in your workplace because of what makes you different from those around you. We start with your name because names are powerful. In this chapter, I'm going to walk you through the process of tapping into that power. First, we're going to take a moment to think about the meaning and use of names so we can understand why they are so important.

What I love about "Who am I?" is that it's a simple question that yields fast and often unexpected results. When I'm coaching a client to own their Imposter Syndrome and we start work on their Imposter Speech, this question often surprises them. They're not expecting to spend the whole first session talking about their name. But when we start to delve deeper into what their name stands for, the relationship they have with their name and how they use it, they realise something they have been overlooking for years: their name is a powerful confidence anchor and the secret to creating confidence in the moment.

_____

BERNADETTE'S STORY

Take Bernadette, for example. Bernadette contacted me on the eve of starting her new job as a senior manager at a global accounting firm. As you'd expect when starting a new position, Bernadette was excited about her new role and keen to make a good first impression. But she was also anxious; anxious about fitting into the culture of the organisation, which wasn't exactly known for its diversity credentials, and worried about the homegrown talent that she was being asked to lead. Her coaching objective was simple: to "sort out" her Imposter Syndrome so she could stop holding herself back and be more confident about her own value.

My first session with Bernadette took place just two weeks into her new role. As you'd expect, she'd already attended a number of internal meetings to discuss various projects. In addition, Bernadette had been working hard to introduce herself to as many people as possible and start building relationships. This meant she'd had many opportunities to say her name and we had plenty of examples and experiences to work with.

Bernadette's full name is Bernadette Cooper[13]. But if you'd met her before we started working together, it would take

you a while to know this because she would have introduced herself as Bernadette in a voice you could hardly
hear and with all the enthusiasm of a disillusioned waitress
who is pretending she is here to help. Hearing her say her
name gave you the distinct impression she neither wanted
you to hear it or remember it.

The name Bernadette Cooper has five syllables and is
packed with powerful consonants. It's a beautiful strong
name with a lyrical rhythm that is crying out to be heard
and remembered. But a name doesn't achieve this by
itself. It needs to be owned. It needs to be valued by the
person that owns it. And it needs to be communicated
in a way that makes you want to find out more about the
person behind it.

The way Bernadette now introduces herself, and the way
she feels when she does so has completely changed as a
result of the work we did together around the first step
of the Imposter Speech, "*Who am I?*" She says her name
clearly, audibly and confidently because she now under-
stands the power that a name has – not only to communicate value and make it easy for others to remember
you, but also to make you feel confident and self-assured. Instead of feeling indifferent about her name, she
now feels emboldened by it. Within weeks, Bernadette
reported that saying her name aloud had become a kind
of confidence trigger that she uses as often as she can. It

was empowering. Saying her name made her feel confident and capable in that moment.

Why your name helps build a stronger identity

Your name helps build a stronger identity because it is the entry point to who you are. It is the symbol of your identity which, when used with intention and the weight of your Imposter Speech behind it (I'll explain how this works in Chapter 14), has the potential to become the only confidence tool you'll ever need. This may sound too simple to be true, but trust me, it is so much more than you think it is when you casually offer it up at a first encounter, or fill it out on the first line of a written form. Your name is the distillation of who you are.

The idea that names are important is nothing new. They have long been recognised as the cornerstones of autonomy and identity. This is why, when autocratic regimes want to disempower or dehumanise someone, one of the first things they do is take away their name. Prisoners of war, Holocaust victims, slaves – erasing a person's name (or replacing it with yours) is a powerful weapon of subjugation. When our name is taken away our sense of self is at risk.

Conversely, being given a name is the beginning of our identity. It's what gives us a sense of self. Most likely,

"

*Your name is
the distillation of
who you are.*

"

your parents spent months agonising over which name to choose for you – conscious that the name will form the basis of your identity. Even if you are from a culture where children's names are pre-determined by their family line, place of birth or paternal or maternal nomenclature, the choice for your name was still carefully considered. Even excited parents-to-be who choose not to burden their child with a name of too much significance consciously make that decision.

Paul and I fell into this latter category. The names Paul and I chose for our boys – Dylan, Noah, Luca and Maxwell – were largely random. After a brief flirtation with the idea of choosing names that resonated with who we were and where we were from, we decided it would be so much easier to just find a name we liked. So Dylan came to us as a process of elimination; Noah was always going to be Noah; Luca – Italian-born – was an Italian name we'd always found appealing; and Maxwell, well, it took a while to find Max! We were fast running out of boys' names and settled on taking inspiration from the soul singer Maxwell that we'd listened to over and over again in the first year we dated.

As a child, one of the first sounds you learned to respond to was your name. Research shows that from a very young age, several regions in the left hemisphere of the brain show greater activation to the sound of our own name compared to when we hear other people's names. Your name then, scientists conclude, is one of the first markers of self-identification. In light of this, it's only fitting that it becomes a marker for your self-confidence.

IMPOSTER TRUTH

Most people I have met and worked with have not given any thought to the idea of owning their name as a symbol (like a national flag) of who they are.

So, who are you?

Being asked your name seems like the simplest of questions. Don't be fooled. Beneath that question lies an opportunity for self-exploration that, if your life is as busy as mine, is a rare and welcome one. It's asking you to shine a light on yourself as if for the first time, so you can see yourself with fresh non-judgemental eyes. Before we get to creating this part of your speech, let's take a look at your relationship with your name today.

How do you feel about your name?

Have you ever considered the significance of your name and what you communicate to yourself and the world in the way you say it? I have to confess – before doing this

work for the first time as part of my own imposter transformation, I had never considered it. My name was something that, in a work environment, came bumbling reck-
lessly out of my mouth while my attention was distracted
by the thought of what I needed to say next in order to
hide my Imposter Syndrome. Meanwhile, in my personal
life, I barely gave it a second thought. As far as names
go, Caroline Heath (my maiden name) was not a name
to either evoke confidence in its owner or spark curiosity
in the listener. (Or at least, that was how I thought at the
time.) Then, when I married Paul in 2004 and the question
of whether I'd keep Heath or switch to Flanagan came up,
I was borderline indifferent. After a half-hearted attempt
to hold onto my maiden name at work, the minor irrita-
tion of having a different surname to our baby son Dylan,
and Paul's growing frustration at being called "Mr Heath"
when we would check in to a hotel on holiday (which I
found a lot funnier than Paul did), I decided it was all getting far too complicated. "In for a penny, in for a pound!"
I believe was my somewhat cavalier attitude at the time.
And I quite enjoyed witnessing the look of bemusement
on people's faces when the Caroline Flanagan they met
in person turned out not to be a porcelain-skinned, fair-
haired Irish girl with a lyrical lilting accent, but a black girl
of Jamaican descent with whatever you call an accent that
starts in Birmingham, matures in London and has sprin-
klings of Kent and Cambridge. I had no idea that my rela-

tionship with my name held the secret to greater confidence and personal power, or that it could be the symbol of my identity. Neither did I appreciate that how I say my name was a cue that others take from me about who I am or hint at the value I had to offer.

Now, thanks to my Imposter Speech (not just the process of creating it, but the regular use of it – more on the importance of this in Chapter 15), my relationship with my name could not be more different. I love my name. I am fiercely proud of it and consider it a precious asset. Like Bernadette, I instantly feel more capable and more in control when I say it. It grounds me, centres me. Beneath "My name is Caroline Flanagan" lies not just power but also possibility. It is the opposite of the not-being-enough of my old imposter identity.

How do you say your name?

Look closely enough, and you'll see the truth of this elsewhere. Now I have to tell you, I'm a James Bond fan. I know James Bond movies are cheesy and implausible, but, I love them. What I especially love, what I spend the whole movie waiting for, is the moment that occurs in every Bond movie where Bond (preferably Daniel Craig, hopefully someday soon, Idris Elba) is asked: "Who are you?" There's the inevitable pause. And then the inimitable response: "The name's Bond. James Bond." It is predictable and cringey and almost always over the top, but there is no escaping the power and gravitas of that moment. It's as if the whole movie is designed around that moment. As if the director started with that statement and then filled the rest of the story in around the edges of that moment. All Bond is doing is saying his name. But when you hear the words "James Bond" you don't just hear a name, you hear a whole personality, an attitude and a life story. In those two words, you hear how many times he's had a brush with death but escaped, how often he's saved the world just in the nick of time, how many times he's charmed and seduced his leading lady. You hear that he's not afraid to break the rules, but only if it's to do the right thing, and how he's never going to let himself be intimidated and that he'll stop at nothing to put things right. And all he did was say his name.

But look closer and there's more. When James Bond says his name, he's not just sending a message to anyone who'll listen. He is also sending that same strong statement of identity that evokes who he is to himself. He is empowering himself.

The question then becomes, not what does your name say about you, but what does your name say to you? Or better still, what does your name do for you?

How do you communicate your name?

When we start to realise how powerful names can be, it becomes clear how much we take our name for granted. Unlike my 007 hero, we mumble them, shorten them, whisper them and gloss over them. When we say our name or introduce ourselves, we are mostly absent – spewing out the words without emotion or meaning, our minds too busy calculating what we want to say or do next to consider the power and significance of our names. With our often careless disregard for names, is it any wonder others are quick to shorten or assign us nicknames without our consent, or that our names are quickly forgotten when we leave the room?

Does this resonate? Think about the last networking event you attended. How clearly do you think you introduced yourself to those you met? Did you speak slowly and clearly enough for them to hear? If so, how do you know? Do you think they would remember your name after the event? This raises an interesting point about whose responsibility it is when it comes to people remembering our names. Almost everyone I meet comments on their struggle with remembering names. It's true we need to pay better attention to other people's names when we hear them. But we also need to pay better attention to our names when we say them. Perhaps then our names would be easier for others to remember.

How you communicate your name becomes especially important when you think about pronunciation. If you are a person of colour, you may have a name that Westerners find challenging to pronounce correctly. How much thought have you put into saying your name in a way that is clearly understood, and how well do you communicate the powerful message of who you are in the way you introduce yourself? If this is something you have worked on, then very good for you. But if the only time you think about your name is when it's misspelt or mispronounced then it's time for a change of tack.

Think about the last time you introduced yourself. How clearly or audibly did you speak? What intonation did you use? What message did you send with the tone and speed of that communication? How much responsibility did you take for ensuring that your name was heard, understood and could easily be pronounced and remembered? Sometimes, we expect others to pay more attention to our names than we do ourselves.

Do you like your name?

Before you can start using your name as a confidence aid and realising its power, it's important to look at your current relationship with your name.

Do you like your name?

Do you feel connected to it?

This may seem a trivial consideration but it's an important one. Not everyone likes their name. Most of us are walking around with names we didn't choose. But while the majority of us grow into our names and learn to inhabit them, for some, their name is a point of tension within themselves.

What matters is not the name, but how that name contributes to your sense of identity, the outward message of who you are and the internal message that you want to send to yourself. It's not the name itself, but your connection with it and the power you derive from it that counts.

For this part of your speech to work, it is vitally important that you learn to like your name. And I don't mean tolerate your name. I mean LOVE your name. Love your name so much it could be splashed across the billboards in Piccadilly Circus and you'd beam with pride. Love it so much just hearing it makes you feel better.

It's not uncommon for a person of African descent to love their name and then arrive in the US and experience so much pushback and judgement about their name that they start to question it and see it as a weapon of alienation and isolation. Or for a person of Indian descent to hear their name mispronounced and mimicked and shortened to such an extent that a previously loved name becomes a source of shame. If this is you, and there is even one iota of shame or insecurity over your name, this is the work you need to do.

The Imposter Speech is here to help you. To own who you are and how you want to be identified. The answer is to take ownership and responsibility for your name. You want to get to the point where you can appreciate the power of your name enough to transcend other people's mistakes, where you can correct or educate them without being defensive, without anger or judgement, but with authority and confidence.

How do you react when people get your name wrong?

If you have a name that is unfamiliar to the Western workplace, you are probably used to having people get it wrong. What comes up for you when this happens? What are you making it mean? It's easy to feel disrespected and undervalued when others mispronounce your name, but when you do this you're giving away your power. It's OK to insist that others get your name right as a sign of respect, but your confidence should not depend on it. Your confidence should be solid enough to transcend it. This is exactly what the Imposter Speech is going to help you achieve.

Your name is an anchor

Answering the question, *"Who am I?"* had powerful results for me immediately. I experienced this in a variety of situations – from the simple act of answering the phone (always, in responding to an unknown number, my first words are "Caroline Flanagan" or "Caroline Flanagan speaking") to providing my name to the DPD parcel courier who asks me to confirm my name. Each time that I said it I was reinforcing my sense of self, and it gave me such a boost. And nowhere is this more powerful than in my talks. The opening lines of my keynotes are never about me (my priority is to speak directly to you and let you know you're in the right room) but soon after my first few sentences, I come to a brief introduction to who I am. This has a profound effect and is a great tip if you want to anchor yourself in a presentation. Deliver a powerful opening to grab your audience's attention and set the tone, and then when you're a few minutes in, introduce yourself with confidence using your name. It will ground you and anchor you. It acts as my compass in the early part of my keynote when the adrenaline is still pumping and I'm still feeling anxious. It can be as powerful for you too, both in your personal life and in your professional life. And the beauty of this is that it's not just when you say it that it gives you power. For the whole time in between, it's working in the background, building your confidence. How this works will become clearer as we work our way through the Imposter Speech. Before we get to that, let's move onto creating your statement.

Who am I? – The Process

Now that you understand just how significant your name is, it's time to turn your own name into a powerful source of confidence for you. First, the process. Below is a list of tasks I use with my clients to guide them through this process. You can work through these tasks on your own at home. (You can download a free sheet to help you do this via this link: **www.carolineflanagan.com/imposter-speech.**) But if you like the idea of getting inspiration and accountability from others, you can also work through this as part of a group (for details of my Imposter programme, go to **www.carolineflanagan.com/imposterspeech/join**).

TASKS

1. Start and end each day by greeting yourself with your name

Greet yourself every morning, out loud, and preferably in the mirror, and do the same last thing at night. To make this easy to remember, try to tag this new task onto the end of a well-established habit. This is called habit stacking, and is a great way to introduce new routines and disciplines into your life. In this case, a great habit to pin your greeting to is brushing your teeth. As you put down your toothbrush, look at yourself in the mirror, give a million-dollar smile and say good morning or good night to yourself. If you really want to have fun with this, add a wink! You may want to scoff at this but it's guaranteed to make you laugh and will ensure you don't take yourself too seriously. The more fun you can have with this, the better and more effective it will be. Make sure you use your name (you want to be hearing it all the time) every time and say it like you mean it, and as if you love it. Look yourself in the eye and speak up. For the 20 seconds it takes to complete this task, be totally present.

2. Experiment with how you say it and find the emphasis you like the most

Most first names and surnames, taken together, amount to several syllables, which means there are different ways of saying them. You can emphasise different syllables and put the stress in different places. Caroline Flanagan could be *Caro*line *Flana*gan with the emphasis on the two first syllables. But it could also be Caro*line* Flana*gan*. Or Ca*ro*line Fla*na*gan. How many different ways could you say your name? When you've exhausted all the possibilities your name offers, add the prefixes you'd use to introduce yourself "My name is" or "I am" and play around with different ways of saying that. "My *name* is Caroline Flanagan" sounds quite different to "My name *is* Caroline Flanagan". There's no right or wrong way to say your name. It's your name after all! What you are doing here is trying on different ways of saying it to see which of them you like the most. This is simply a question of personal preference. You're looking for a way of saying your name that feels good when you say it. Don't be in a rush to decide. Try different versions when you're out and about and introducing yourself. After a short while, there'll be a clear winner – the way of saying your name that feels the most natural and effective.

3. Articulate every sound and soften it with a smile

Now it's time to think about clarity. Do you rush the sounds in your name so that they become jumbled together? When it comes to words we are familiar with, it's easy to rush through them and lose the sounds in the process. At one point, "Caroline Flanagan" began to sound like "Carline Flanagan" and I noticed that people would often ask me to repeat my name. If people often ask you to repeat your name, it may be more of an indicator of your communication skills than it is of their listening skills. So slow things down. Take the time to wrap your lips around the consonants in your name, and put your tongue to work on those vowels. Every sound is there for a reason. In addition, smile when you say your name. If smiling and saying your name involves too much in the way of lip gymnastics then let your lips do the talking and smile instead with your eyes.

4. "Shazam" your name

I want you to imagine that every time you say your name you're unleashing a little more of its power. The use of repetition to give power to a name is nothing new. There are movies, myths and legends where names are repeated and used as powerful incantations. If you're as old as I am, you'll remember the haunting 1992 horror movie *Candyman* in which a terrifying killer could be summoned by repeating his name five times in the mirror (the memory of watching this movie as a kid still haunts me, so I will not be watching the sequel which is due for release in 2020!).

There's also *Shazam!* the superhero film in which 14-year-old Billy is transported to another dimension and meets the ancient wizard Shazam who chooses the boy as his new champion. By saying "Shazam!" three times, Billy is transformed into an adult superhero. What if saying your name could transform you into a superhero? Why shouldn't it? Have fun with this. The more fun you have, the better. I want you laughing in the mirror as you say it. Swivel round as if you're James Bond, fake gun in hand, and say it like you mean it.

5. Say your full name as often as possible

As you go about your day, see how many times you can say your full name. Answering the door, answering the phone, introducing yourself – find as many opportunities as you can. Make sure you do say your full name. I ask my clients to make it a rule to use their full name, even in circumstances when others are using first names. Many people fear that using their full name will sound too distant and make them feel unapproachable. But I've found that by smiling as I say my name, this doesn't happen. I may stand out from others. But I consider this a good thing. Another trick I use to avoid the risk of creating distance is to ask the other person's surname, so it's more of an equal exchange. My excuse for this is that I'll find them and their name much easier to remember (or find online so we can connect) if I have the surname too.

6. Tackle the pronunciation issue

We've already talked about the issue of name pronunciation in Part II. For you, this may be a sensitive subject which can compound your Imposter Syndrome and trigger feelings of being disrespected and undervalued. By now, hopefully, you are beginning to take much greater ownership of your name, which includes taking more responsibility for how others pronounce it. Remember, simply expecting others to get your name right (or even to remember it after only hearing it once) because it's the respectful thing to do is all very well, but it's giving other people far too much power over your emotions. If they get it wrong, you are frustrated and angry and resentful.

Do you have a shorter version you are happy to use? If not, how can you help others to say your name? What does it sound like? What image will help them to pronounce or remember it? For example, "My name is... but you can call me/everyone calls me..." I'm able to pronounce Chimamanda Ngozi Adichie with reasonable confidence only because she is a renowned African author whose name I have read and heard spoken aloud many times. If I had

had the pleasure of meeting her in person before knowing of her, and she had introduced herself casually and inaudibly as most people do, I would struggle. I'd need her help. Yes, it is my job to care. But it is also yours to show me how.

7. Prepare for when someone says your name wrong

How can you respectfully correct them? Try different strategies. For example, if your name is Kamala, like the new US vice president, and people repeatedly call you Camilla, or pronounce your name Kamala, with the emphasis on the second a, you could say: "It's Kamala. Just think of 'calmer' and 'la' and put the two together." Or "You're not the first person to call me Camilla. But it's Kamala. Just notice how calm I'm being about you getting my name wrong, and that will remind you" and "No seriously, it's my name, and names matter. It's important that you get it right." Test them out and see what's most effective.

8. Pay better attention to other people's names

How well do you remember them? How well do you listen when others tell you their name? We typically focus on ourselves when we're engaged in others. That's why we struggle to remember people's names. The aim of this is to increase your awareness of how other people use their names, and make you more alert to how you use yours.

Who am I? – The Speech

Now we are going to create and practise the first line of your Imposter Speech. Say your name as if you are introducing yourself. But don't just say it. Remember what we've discussed and say it like you mean it.

"My name is Caroline Flanagan."

How to take this further

Being able to embrace and say your name with ease, confidence, gravitas and in a way that empowers you may feel awkward at first. Don't expect it to come easily. In fact, if it does, it means you're not going far enough. To ensure you're really challenging yourself and receive more support, this is a great exercise to do with a buddy or in a group. In addition to the individuals I coach on this, I also deliver Imposter Speech workshops to help people with creating their speech[14] and it's amazing how powerful (and entertaining!) it is when people do this in a group, and are both challenging and supporting each other.

Summary

- The first step of the Imposter Speech is *"Who am I?"*

- The answer to this question is simple: your name.

- Knowing who you are helps with Imposter Syndrome because it switches your focus away from everything you are not (in comparison with others), and redirects it to everything you are.

- Repeating your name helps build a stronger identity because it is the distillation of who you are and serves as a powerful symbol of your identity.

- Create the first statement in your Imposter Speech by writing your name and then saying it with intention.

WHERE AM I?

"I think it pisses God off if you walk by the color purple in a field somewhere and don't notice it."

- ALICE WALKER

In the previous chapter, we looked at the first step of the Imposter Speech: "*Who am I?*" We discussed how your name is one of the most powerful and, until now, underutilised tools for personal empowerment. I showed you the process for building a powerful connection to your name so that your answer to the question "*Who am I?*" becomes a trigger for feeling more confident, in control and stepping into your power. You created a short powerful identity statement that will form the first line of your Imposter Speech.

As a result of the work you've done so far, you may already be feeling different. Like Bernadette, you may already be using your name to help you feel more confident. But this is only the beginning.

What is the second step in the Imposter Speech?

In this chapter, we look at the second step of the Imposter Speech: "*Where am I?*" This step is about the successes you have had in the past, which you have forgotten, undermined or been far too quick to move on from and the success you are living right now, which you think is all down to luck.

At the end of this chapter, you'll create a powerful statement that is evocative of all you have achieved. You'll then add this to your "*Who am I?*" statement and practise saying these statements together and out loud. Don't be surprised if you already start to feel different as a result of doing so. After completing this step of their Imposter Speech, as part of a group programme or through 1:1 coaching, many clients experience a sudden surge of confidence and feed back to me how different they are beginning to feel.

The purpose of this step is to get you to internalise your past successes and learn how to show up to the next challenge from where you are today. As you know from Chapter 2, this is something which Imposter Syndrome sufferers find hard to do. That's why the second step of your Imposter Speech is dedicated to reflecting on how success has shown up in your life in the past (in all forms) and learning how to separate the success itself from the thoughts, fears and judgements that you have been using to undermine them. As a result of doing this work, you will feel differently about past achievements. These will no longer feel like flukes or accidents – things that have happened to you by chance. They will start to feel like true results that have been created by you.

How knowing where you are helps with your Imposter Syndrome

We start with your successes because being unable to internalise your success is one of the key symptoms of your Imposter Syndrome. You think to yourself: "I shouldn't be here" followed by a catalogue of reasons why: "it's all down to luck, which is going to run out any minute now"; "they think I'm someone I'm not"; and "they think I can do this but they're wrong". Sometimes, this type of questioning is compounded by the fact that the culture where you work may be very different to where you feel most at home (in your family or your community) – sparking thoughts such as, "I don't belong here" and "this isn't the place for me". When your brain is crowded with thoughts of luck running out and not belonging, is it any wonder you struggle to internalise your successes and gain confidence from them?

IMPOSTER TRUTH

Most people with Imposter Syndrome are in such a hurry to move onto the next achievement, they forget to cash in on the rewards of past successes.

Why revisiting past successes helps build a stronger identity

Revisiting past successes creates a stronger identity because it helps you internalise them and digest their rewards. It also teaches you the importance of pausing between achievements going forward. This means stopping for long enough to recognise your achievements as they happen, and being present where you are, rather than relentlessly pursuing the next achievement before you've had time to cash in the confidence that you've earned from earlier ones. As you get better at setting aside your fears and self-judgement around each success, your fear of exposure will gradually give way to a growing confidence in your ability to create more success.

Coaching my clients to internalise their successes is one of my favourite jobs as a coach. Every client I have worked with on this has revealed many more successes than they realised they had. While some clients have simply taken their achievements for granted, others have simply forgotten things they have achieved. Have you ever looked back on an old set of photographs and been reminded of an experience you had completely forgotten about? It's amazing how easily it happens, particularly if you are a high potential person of colour who has been operating at a high level most of your life. You're so preoccupied with fighting battles in the moment, new successes are quickly consigned to the past.

RUTH'S STORY

Ruth is a prime example. I had a *"Where am I?"* session with Ruth after she attended one of my talks on Imposter Syndrome. Ruth is tall and gregarious and the kind of person you warm to instantly. She is a designer for one of the tech giants and, at the time of our coaching conversation, had only recently been promoted to a role in an area where she not only felt inexperienced but also had more people to manage. Her Imposter Syndrome lit up. It conjured up thoughts that she had been given the role by mistake, and all manner of reasons for this, including the notion that, as the only person of colour in her group, she was being singled out and set up to fail. But, not one to accept defeat, Ruth was determined to prove a point. She was working late into the night going over her university notes; reading manuals and scouring the web for articles on how to do her new job. The only problem was that Ruth was exhausted and reaching saturation point. Her acute fear of getting it wrong plus the additional hours she was putting in on top of her already demanding workday were causing her sleepless nights and considerable stress.

I invited Ruth to explore *"Where am I?"* and asked her to tell me about her successes, starting with her recent promotion, with complete objectivity. Her first answer completely failed the test. She mentioned the promotion, but just couldn't stop herself from telling me that she had no idea how she'd got it.

"Just tell me about where you are now," I said, "without telling me what you think about how you got there." And then I sat back and listened. Hesitantly at first, and then after gentle prodding, more willingly, Ruth began to catalogue her achievements and successes. These ranged from her recent promotion to the various titles and responsibilities she had had on the way. Whenever she tried to stop, I'd prompt her with a powerful coaching question: "What else have you done?", which I followed with, "Tell me about another success you supposedly didn't deserve." Each time she'd find something new to say. On her list was a huge range of achievements – from taking responsibility for getting her three younger siblings to school each morning to travelling through Asia by herself during her year off, to being the most senior black woman in her office. The problem was, Ruth had a problem that I see in many high potential people of colour (which I have recognised in myself in the past): overlooking her achievements ("oh, that was nothing") and not stopping for long enough in the moment of success to reflect and internalise it. By teaching Ruth how to separate the facts from the judgement, and by giving her the space to call up her past successes (and challenge her view of what constitutes a success), I helped Ruth to see herself differently. It was as if she'd found a paper trail to where she is now that made her current success easier to connect to.

How "*Where am I?*" helps you show up from where you are

There are two reasons why "*Where am I?*" is so important. The first, which we have already discussed, relates to your past successes and is about helping you to internalise the successes you have already achieved. The second reason it's important is about what you do from here. "*Where am I?*" teaches you the art of being present so that you can show up from where you are. This matters because when you show up from a place of self-doubt, questioning how deserving you are of your current role or responsibility, it is not only exhausting and stressful, but also means you're less likely to give your best performance and are therefore more likely to create the result you are most afraid of: failure.

As you know, I am a keynote speaker and I frequently deliver talks on Imposter Syndrome to large audiences filled with high performers. The night before a talk, you can bet my mind is buzzing with fear, a veritable hive of self-doubt as I question my right to be talking to such a high calibre audience. Even after years of experience, I worry that I have nothing of value to say and I'm not clever or knowledgeable enough to speak to such an audience. But however real those fears are, I know I have a choice about how I show up. I can step onto the stage as the woman who has nothing valuable to say, or I can step onto the stage as the ex-City lawyer with a lifetime of experience living with Imposter Syndrome, and years of experience empowering high performers to turn their Imposter Syndrome into a strength. It stops being about where I think I should or shouldn't be. When the time comes, my best chance of creating the result I want is to show up from where I am.

"Where am I?" then helps you find the best place to show up from. Most clients, when they sign up for coaching, are in a rush to get to the practical steps of how to get results. They want to know how to raise their profile so they can get promoted or build relationships so they can win more clients. What they don't realise (until I show them in our coaching sessions) is how much their inability to accept

*You need to show
up from where you
are first, and the
results follow from
there.*

where they are is impacting their results. They think they can show up with self-doubt and fear, believing they don't deserve to be where they are, and convince clients to entrust them with work. But action plans and concrete steps won't work if you're showing up from a place you think you don't deserve to be. You need to show up from where you are first, and the results follow from there.

So, where are you?

Exploring the question, "*Where am I?*" offers you an opportunity to see yourself in a kinder, fairer light than you ever have before. I'm giving you permission to let go of your attachment to self-criticism and judgement and abandon your fears of being someone who is considered arrogant or cocky or full of themselves. It's an invitation to explore a world you may not have entered before – your own private world where you can sing your own praises and wear your successes on your sleeve with pride. It's unfamiliar, I know. But aren't you just a little bit curious to find out how it feels? Before we go on to find out, take a moment to consider our attitude to success right now.

What constitutes a success?

We spend a lot of time talking about success (particularly in books like this, which are written to help you have more of it!) but little time defining it. It's worth making a distinction here between the question "what is success?" and "what is a success?" The former calls for a deeper, phil-osophical meaning-of-life type answer, which is not what we are looking for here; the latter is a simple invitation to explore what you've done in the past and decide whether it qualifies as a success. The answer would, under any other circumstances, be a highly subjective one, but for you as an Imposter Syndrome sufferer, it can't be – you simply aren't well practised enough at recognising your successes! To counter this, always try to take a step back when assessing what qualifies as a success. "If your best friend had done this, would you consider it a success?" is a very effective question to help clients be more objective.

Who gets to decide?

A second and related point to consider when recalling your success is who gets to decide. A common trait in Imposter Syndrome sufferers, which I see in almost every one of my clients (and have been guilty of myself in the past), is a heavy reliance on external validation. In other words, you need someone in authority, or whose opinion you value, to tell you that something is a success before you can see it for yourself. Sound familiar? Watch out for this. While it's great to receive positive feedback and rec-ognition for the work you have done, relying on others to diagnose your successes is giving way too much of your power away to other people. This book is about finding more of your power and stepping boldly into it, and this exercise on your past successes is going to help you do that. A powerful way to challenge your dependence on external validation going forward, and one I use personally all the time now, is to decide on my success criteria ahead of time.

By way of example, here are my success criteria for this book (phrased as questions to leave no room for ambiguity or doubt):

- Did I get it done?

- Did I get it published and send it out into the world?

- Did I show up as I am so the reader gets to know the real me?

- Did I have the courage to say what I believe?

- Did I speak to the reader?

- Did I share my own experiences?

- Did I put my heart and soul and everything I had into it?

- When I see someone else pick up the book to read it, will I feel proud of what they'll find inside?

You'll note that everything in this list is within my control. This is significant because it puts my success within my control, so it's not about external validation. Now don't get me wrong, I'm not saying external validation isn't important to me and shouldn't be important to you. What you won't see on the front cover of this book, if you are one of its first readers (but you may see someday, when there's a new print run) are the words "International Bestseller" and "over a million copies sold", but these words have been written on the front page of the draft of this book since the first day that I sat down at my desk, opened up a blank Word document and asked myself: where should I start? Achieving international bestseller status and selling a million copies is my goal (if you've bought this copy, thank you for bringing me one step closer; if you've bought one for a friend, double thanks!). It would be an incredible achievement and amazing validation that I would welcome with open arms and tears in my eyes. But that's not a success I can control. I can influence it, but I can't make it happen. So I'm not giving all my power away by relying on others to tell me it's a success. As long as I've ticked all my own boxes, I get to claim my success either way and so should you. Set your success criteria ahead of time so you too can claim your own successes.

How long do you wait before you rush to the next goal?

As someone with Imposter Syndrome, you don't spend nearly enough time celebrating or processing your successes. We discussed the reason for this in Chapter 1. Imposter Syndrome is a unique form of self-doubt because, unlike normal self-doubt, the more you achieve, the worse your Imposter Syndrome gets. As a result, each success simply worsens your Imposter Syndrome and drives the need for more success. You don't have the luxury of basking in the glory of what you've just achieved. You're too busy rushing to the next achievement.

The way I describe this to my clients is by comparing it to going out to a wonderful restaurant. You eat a beautiful meal, and then as soon as you've finished, instead of stopping to digest what you've eaten, absorb its nutrients, bask momentarily in the pleasurable aftermath of feeling satisfied and fulfilled, you rush straight out to another restaurant and do the same all over again! Is this you?

How do you feel about your current role?

A key part of *"Where am I?"* is recognising your current role or title. How do you feel about this? Does the title or role mean something to you? Does it reflect the work you do? The relationship between you and your role is a key one. If you feel it doesn't reflect your value or contribution, it's probably a source of frustration or tension. It also means you may struggle with the call to "show up from where you are".

INDIA'S STORY

One of my clients is a salaried partner in a prestigious law firm, which means she is effectively the second tier from the top (at the top sit the equity partners). I noticed after a few coaching sessions together that she kept referring to herself and, by implication, the other salaried partners as "not a real partner". She felt that while the equity partners were the real deal, the salaried partners were not. In her mind, she and her fellow salaried partners were less deserving and less credible. As part of the work we are doing together I am helping her to have a little more respect for her success in achieving a level of success that, as she herself admitted, many highly impressive and accomplished lawyers have been unsuccessful in achieving. The message here isn't "be grateful for what you have", it's "show some respect for where you are".

Do you compare your success to others?

It's hard to celebrate past successes and where you are today if you are constantly comparing yourself to others. It's easy to do – particularly when you work in an environment where competition between peers is encouraged. If you are someone who constantly compares yourself to others, be aware that this will compromise your ability to see your successes for the achievements they are. Be mindful of those two or three other work colleagues you are constantly comparing yourself to (we all have them!). This is your world and these are your successes. They have no business being in it.

Are you hiding from your successes?

As Imposter Syndrome sufferers, we sometimes hide from our successes. Do you have a success in the closet that you are pretending not to have? Is there a success that you are so disconnected from, it causes you discomfort to even think about? If there are places you want to avoid in your exploration of past successes, this is where you need to go. Leave no stone unturned. Your hidden successes may lead to a powerful transformation. They did for me.

THE RELUCTANT ALUMNUS

It's June 2019 and I am standing outside Corpus Christi College, Cambridge. I'm here to attend the Bacon Law Society dinner for college alumni. What makes this visit remarkable is the fact that it is only my second visit to Corpus since I graduated 24 years previously. It has taken me this many years to accept that I was a Cambridge alumnus.

It turns out that one of the ways my Imposter Syndrome likes to manifest itself is in the alumni world. I have it with being an alumnus at my secondary school, Cranbrook, and I have it with Cambridge. I had it with Allen & Overy when I left in 2002 (I attended my first alumni event 15 years later in 2017), and I had it with Cleary Gottlieb, the law firm I worked at after Allen & Overy, which I left in 2005 (I have attended one event in 15 years). It's no coincidence that the places where I have struggled to return as an alumnus are the places where I have felt most like an imposter. I stayed on the alumni mailing list and always knew what was going on. I'd receive invitations to all the events. But, each time I considered it, the thought of going back filled me with such fear and dread, I came up with a hundred excuses not to attend. I felt I had been lucky to avoid exposure as a fraud while I was there. Going back as one of the alumni was simply too big a risk. What if I was exposed this time around?

I have *"Where am I?"* to thank for my transformation in this area. It forced me to confront, and own, a success I had been avoiding for years, even though the fact of me having attended those places has been visible for all to see (on my LinkedIn profile, for example). As a result of doing this work, it is so much easier to show up to my work as a coach and keynote speaker to high achievers like you. I'm no longer squandering my energy on the fear of not being enough. I've internalised my past achievements and can now show up from where I am and be 100% focused on doing what I came here to do.

Where am I? – The Process

This process will help you recall as many successes and achievements in your life as possible so that you have an exhaustive list. The act of producing this list is a journey in and of itself. It will take you to places and achievements you have long forgotten or taken for granted. (Remember there's a free downloadable sheet to help you do this here – **www.carolineflanagan.com/imposterspeech**).

TASKS

1. 100 successes

Take a blank sheet of paper and brainstorm 100 successes you have achieved in your life to date. One hundred may sound like a big ask, but there's a good reason for choosing such a high number. I want to really challenge you to look beyond the most recent and most obvious successes that come easily to mind. The whole point of this exercise is to take you further than you would go by yourself. Also, try to be as specific as you can. The more detail you can recall the better. In Chapter 3, I talked about remembering that I'd won the Viney Music Prize at school. That memory took me back to the day of the prize-giving. I can remember being in the main hall of the school and my name being called, as well as the clapping and my nervousness and excitement when I went up to collect the prize. And then I remembered the Christian Endeavour Prize I won and the Prize for Extra-Curricular Activities and the Form Prize and the Art Prize etc. (I told you I was an overachiever!) and just how amazing that last Speech Day was. I found myself looking back on my younger self with a new-found sense of awe and respect. Reliving the actual memory of your success is a really important part of this exercise. The more you can re-experience those successes, the more powerful the effect of this exercise will be on your confidence.

To help you answer, *"Where am I?" here* are some of the questions I use with my clients:

- What are you most proud of?

- What do you remember as your first success?

- What would you say is your greatest achievement?

- What success or achievement have you left off your LinkedIn profile because you don't think they add value?

- Where are you in your career right now?

- What's the hardest thing you have ever done?

- Which of your achievements most surprises you?

- What are you known for?

- What else?

It's a good idea to get help with these questions, especially if your Imposter Syndrome is particularly acute. But when you ask other people what they think your achievements are, be mindful that you're not asking them to do this work for you. You just want their help remembering successes that you've forgotten and recognising successes you have previously taken for granted.

- What would others say was your greatest achievement?

- What success do you feel you least deserve?

- Which achievement causes you the most anxiety right now?

One of the issues you might stumble across is what constitutes a success or an achievement. It's easy to recognise your achievement when it comes with a title, a pay rise or an award. But don't overlook what may appear to be less noteworthy achievements in your life, or the ones you take for granted. For example:

- Achieving a personal best.

- Being a mother or father.

- Staying the distance long after you wanted to quit.

- Having the courage to make a difficult decision.

- Stepping out of your comfort zone.

- Learning something new.

Even if you are unsure of whether something is a success or achievement, write it down. We're going to take a look at your thoughts about it next.

2. Separate the facts from your thoughts

The next step is to sort your successes and achievements into two columns (if you're using the free worksheet, this will be easy). In the first column, write only the facts. In the second column, write down any thoughts you have about those facts. As you search for your successes, your brain will want to qualify and judge them. It will want to eliminate achievements that don't seem particularly impressive to you, you've seen others do more times or in a better way. Stay alert. When you hear yourself qualifying, questioning and slipping into judgement, write these down in the second column, so they are separate from the facts.

IMPOSTER TRUTH

When asked to think about your achievements, your imposter brain will want to tell you all about your failures. Make a note of them. Park them aside for now. (We'll come to those in Step 4.)

3. Sit with your achievements

If this is the first time you've allowed yourself to reflect on your achievements, it may trigger certain feelings and emotions. I know for me, the memory of getting a training contract at Allen & Overy is an emotional one. It was such a meaningful achievement because from that moment on, I knew I could earn enough money to pay my own rent, and I would therefore never be evicted again. If recalling your past or present successes brings up emotions for you, allow it. Releasing any emotions that come up is all part of the process.

Where am I? – The Speech

Now that you have your list of successes and achievements, it's time to create the one liner[15] for your speech by reviewing your list and selecting those successes that symbolise your greatest achievements to date. Don't allow yourself to get stuck here. None of this is fixed and you can change this as often as you need to until you create something that works for you. It's important to see your Imposter Speech as a work in progress that you are constantly refining and adapting to your circumstances and challenges. There are no right or wrong answers. Just pick the achievements that resonate most with you today and try them on for size.

Add your answer to the first line of your Imposter Speech which you created in Step 1 and practise saying them repeatedly and out loud so that you internalise their message.

"My name is Caroline Flanagan.

I am an ex-City lawyer who is now a transformational coach, inspirational speaker, twice an author and mother of four boys."

How to take this further

Some people love this exploration into past achievements and complete this step with ease. Others, meanwhile, find it quite challenging. This was certainly the case for me, as it brought up a lot of "stuff" (some of which I have shared in Chapter 2) from when I was growing up. In either case, it's worth considering doing this exercise as part of a group or with a partner. While your Imposter Speech is for you and you alone, the process of creating it can be enriched by the feedback you receive from others (whether that is part of one of my Imposter workshops or my group coaching programme[16] or, with a friend on the same journey).

Summary

» The second step of the Imposter Speech is *"Where am I?"*

» The answer to this question can be found by revisiting past successes and being present with where you are now.

» Revisiting past successes gives you the opportunity to internalise your achievements and digest their rewards.

» Being present with where you are now, your current position or title, for example, helps you to show up from where you are.

» Create the second statement of your Imposter Speech by reviewing your list of successes and selecting those which represent your greatest achievements to date.

WHY AM I HERE?

"He who has a why to live for can bear almost any how."

– FRIEDRICH NIETZSCHE

In the last chapter, we looked at Step 2 of the Imposter Speech: *"Where am I?"* which is all about recalling and internalising your past successes so that you feel more connected to where you are now. You also learned how to be present with where you are (your current success) without questioning or judgement, so that you can show up to the next challenge with more confidence and better focus. By the end of Step 2, you had a powerful success statement to add the second layer of confidence to your Imposter Speech.

If you've done the work of the last two chapters, you'll already be experiencing the benefits of the Imposter

Speech, even though there is more to come. There is a power in repeating your name, and in sifting through your past for the golden nuggets of successes that have been long forgotten or quickly passed over. As your Imposter Speech takes shape, you will start to feel that a new empowered identity is starting to form.

What is the third step in the Imposter Speech?

In this chapter, we look at Step 3 of the Imposter Speech: "*Why am I here?*" The answer to this question can be found by exploring what matters to you most. The result is a list of the core values that drive your behaviour. They are the *why* behind where you are today and what will drive you forward tomorrow.

At the end of this chapter, you'll create a strong statement that evokes the power of your core values so that you are all fired up for the challenges ahead. When you add this to your "*Who am I?*" and "*Where am I?*" statement and hear yourself saying these out loud, you're going to feel the momentum of your Imposter Speech start to build and the way you think about yourself will start to change. As a result of doing this work, you'll have a better understanding of the decisions and choices that have brought you to where you are today and, as a result, you'll feel more confident about your chosen path. You'll understand what drives you and be able to use this knowledge to motivate you through the challenges you'll encounter as you pursue your goals.

How knowing why you are here helps with your Imposter Syndrome

A classic symptom of Imposter Syndrome is questioning your past decisions. This is a common trait amongst my clients and something I can relate to. The pattern is almost always the same. They experience a setback at work that triggers the feeling they don't belong – either something sudden like a rejection ("we won't be putting you forward for promotion this year") or something underlying, like systemic bias in its many forms. *"Why am I here?"* helps you understand the decisions you've made in the past that have brought you to this point. This is particularly important for that stage when you find yourself questioning whether you are in the right job or company or industry. You may have experienced this personally. When things are really challenging at work, it's tempting to look back and question past decisions: "I shouldn't have chosen law" or "Why did I take this job?" or "I fell into banking by accident." This has two negative consequences. The first is that it undermines your confidence to make future decisions. The second is that you may be in too much of a hurry to fix what you think was a bad decision and rush into making a rash decision to try to correct it.

Why knowing your values helps build a stronger identity

Knowing your values helps build a stronger identity because it reveals what matters most to you, and, therefore, what drives your behaviour. As a result, you'll develop an understanding and appreciation of who you are. It will help you see the integrity in your past decisions and, therefore, give you confidence in your ability to make future ones. This is empowering. You're taking responsibility for the decisions that led you to where you are and, as a result, you take on the identity of a person who lives by design and knows how to create results. You are not here by accident, chance or mishap. You are here for a reason, and you know what those reasons are.

Your values are also important because you can use them to make future decisions that align with what matters most to you. The moments in which you are going to need and want to use your Imposter Speech (we'll talk about these in more detail in Chapter 15) are the moments when you have a decision to make: shall I give up on this or should I keep going? Shall I stay on this path or should I change tack? Shall I take a risk or is it better for me to play it safe?

RINA'S STORY

Rina, who is one of the few women, and the only one of Indian descent, in her group in an investment bank, had a similar crisis. There was no failed promotion, just her steady disillusionment with an organisation that she felt overlooked her talents and applied a different standard to her because she is a woman of colour. Rina came to me for coaching to help her find what she really wanted to do. Although there was scope for progression in her current role, she told me she had always felt a bit of an outsider and was starting to wonder if her decision to work in finance had been wrong from the start. She told me that before taking her current role, she had considered becoming a teacher. She was now starting to consider stepping off the progression treadmill altogether and stepping into what she described as a "more soft and cuddly role". But she was conflicted. She feared that making this move would trigger the judgement and disappointment of her peers and superiors, who would see it as "giving up" and "not being able to handle it". On the other hand, it annoyed Rina that she cared what others thought. "Why do I care what others think?" she asked me. "Why can't I be some- one who can just take a back seat and relax? I wish I was the sort of person who could be satisfied just doing their day job and then coming home and watching TV. But I'm just not able to be like that."

Rina thought she was experiencing a conflict between where she is now (in a high-achieving role suited to ambitious types) and what she believes will make her happy (a supportive nurturing role suited to less ambitious types). It had been her choice to go into finance (she couldn't, unfortunately, put the blame on her parents who had raised her to believe she could be anything she wanted) but now she was starting to wonder if all the ambition and accomplishment of her working life had been a betrayal of her true self. "Maybe I've been in the wrong place all along," she reflected.

The work that I did with Rina around *"Why am I here?"* included coaching her on her core values and how they had influenced her choices to this point. We looked at the past decisions she had made that had taken her down her current career path and the motivations behind them. As Rina was aware, her core values (the things that mattered to her most) included supporting and empowering others. But achievement, leadership and recognition were also core values for Rina. Adventure and challenge were too.

Coaching gave Rina a deeper understanding of who she is and what drives her. She recognised that she is in her current position (a position, I might add, that is not so easily or accidentally arrived at) for a reason: she has always gained great satisfaction and fulfilment from working hard, being challenged and being recognised by both her peers and loved ones for her achievements. Her career and life choices to date hadn't been a mistake. She was exactly where she was supposed to be.

The deeper self-knowledge and understanding Rina gained from her coaching gave her all the clarity she needed to move forward. She realised that beneath her reluctance to progress her current role to leadership lay a fear of being judged for being too ambitious and that she would become "one of those people" – by which she meant a leader who treads all over others to get to the top. I was able to coach Rina past this fear, and help her see that there were other ways to lead and that going forward she could choose her own leadership style.

Thanks to *"Why am I here?"*, Rina realised she didn't have to go elsewhere to honour her values. She decided to stay in her current organisation and commit to reaching the next leadership level. And because she knows her values, she can feel confident about that decision. She still finds her role challenging and demanding, but instead of expending most of her energy questioning her past decisions, she's able to focus on doing what it takes to survive in her role.

"

It's not the hard skills and measurable results that ultimately bring us success, happiness and fulfilment.

"

If, like Rina, you work long busy hours in a high-pressure environment, I'm guessing you haven't found time to do much work on uncovering your values. Maybe the idea has never even occurred to you. If this is the case, I'm not surprised. Typically, the only values you encounter in a corporate setting are splashed across your company's web page and often fleetingly observed or blatantly ignored.

I wish I'd understood the concept of values when I was a lawyer working in the City. I knew I was there because I wanted to have a high-paying, recognised career that would be intellectually challenging and give me the opportunity to progress, but I didn't know that what drove this was the core values of security, achievement, recognition and growth I'd acquired from my past.

It was only after leaving the law that I began to appreciate how much more confidence you feel when you know why you are here. Knowing, for example, that achievement and empowerment and growth are important to me has been a powerful driver for me on so many occasions. There were even times when I struggled while writing this book to find the right words, or when my Imposter Syndrome would rear its head and, in a fit of frustration, I'd ask myself, why am I doing this? *Why am I here?* It's the work I've done in Step 3 of my Imposter Speech that has given me an answer to that question that is powerful enough to put me back on track. Knowing first-hand what a difference this can make makes me even more excited to share this solution with you.

Writing a book that will empower other people of colour to fulfil their potential is one of the greatest achievements I could aim for, and the challenge it presents is also an amazing opportunity for growth. That's why I'm here. And you? Why are you here?

IMPOSTER TRUTH

Many people have no idea of the values that have driven their past decisions, or of how to use those values as a compass going forward to ensure they are on the right track.

So, why are you here?

Exploring the question *"Why am I here?"* Is a great opportunity to get to know yourself and understand what makes you tick. Sadly, self-knowledge of this type is not typically at the top of most people's agenda. One reason for this is because it requires a level of introspection that our busy lives leave little time for. A second reason is because, in a work context at least, we tend to be more heavily focused on the hard skills that create measurable tangible results.

But it's not the hard skills and measurable results that ultimately bring us success, happiness and fulfilment. We've all heard the anecdotes about the hard-working businessman or woman who gets to the end of their life only to be filled with regret for having focused only on the results.

"It's incredibly easy to get caught up in an activity trap, in the busy-ness of life, to work harder and harder at climbing the ladder of success only to discover it's leaning against the wrong wall."

STEVEN COVEY
THE 7 HABITS OF HIGHLY EFFECTIVE PEOPLE

When you know your values, you can feel confident that you can make decisions and choices that will create success for you in the future, rather than feeling that you are drifting along. Now that you are reading this book, why not seize the opportunity to discover your own values, so you can use them as a compass going forward? Before we get to the process of doing this, we first need to check in with where you are now. Here are some questions that will help:

Are you put off by your organisation's values?

Most organisations have their values splashed all over their marketing material as a message to the world that they care about more than just making money. Or they care about how they make money. Or both! For most people, this is their first introduction to the concept of values. This is a shame. The problem is that it often gives values a bad press because organisations don't always live by what they say. Sometimes the lived experience of individual employees is completely at odds with what their employer claims to value. I know this is a common experience in people of colour, and perhaps it's yours? Does your organisation claim to value diversity and inclusion but foster a culture that is anything but? If this is your experience of what it means to have values, you may struggle to believe in them.

The distinction that may help with this is between aspirational values and core values. The former represents the values you are aspiring to live by (as may be the case with your employer). The latter represents who you are at your core. The distinction is an important one. You can choose to take or leave your aspirational values; but your core values effectively choose you: they are there, behind the scenes, influencing your decisions and driving your behaviour whether you like it or not! Which is why it's so important that you're aware of these values and understand them.

How do you make decisions?

My friend Helen loves a dilemma, and it's one of the things I love about her. It all stems from our student days at university when we would sit up chatting into the early hours and she would always have a decision to make. Sometimes a big one like whether to date a particular boy or stay away from him. Other times, it was something totally trivial, such as which top to wear with which pair of jeans. We'd debate these decisions for hours, just for the fun of it, going round in circles and indulging in her confusion and staying up half the night in the way that is so fun to be able to do when you don't have kids and a day job and you live in the same building. But when you're a grown-up decision-making gets harder. The stakes are higher. Should I take this job? Should I start my own business? Should I take this position abroad? Should I resign or stay? Go for the promotion? If you are the sort of person who struggles to make decisions and second-guesses those decisions once you've made them, then "*Why am I here*?" will give you the confidence to make better decisions in less time in the future.

Are you pretending not to be ambitious?

You may not see yourself as ambitious, but if you're reading this book to help you succeed in a white world then you most definitely are! There's a reason why you picked up this book and have read this far. There's a reason why you are frustrated with the systemic bias and your own self-doubt – it's not just about equality and fairness, it's because they are barriers to your success and fulfilling your potential.

I am astonished at how many people of colour are either reluctant to admit to being ambitious or they wish that they weren't. Sometimes the reason for this comes from a fear of being "that person": the ruthless ambitious type who treads all over others to serve their own purposes. To hear me talk more about this fear, listen to episode 73 of the *Caroline Flanagan Podcast: Avoiding Being "That Person"*. But mostly, this resistance to ambition is down to discomfort: you simply don't like the pressure you put on yourself to succeed and achieve. Like Rina above, you wish you could take an easier route. I know this because I used to feel like this myself! Answering *"Why am I here?"* is a great help in this situation. It helps you trace back to where your ambition comes from and understand the important role it has played in your life to this point. This is particularly relevant in people of colour who may have developed a strong sense of ambition, as a result of parents who wanted their children to have access to opportunities and freedoms that they never had. Seeing the *why* behind your ambition helps you to be more accepting of the more challenging path you have chosen, and will help to motivate you to stay on track when you might otherwise be tempted to walk away.

Why am I here? – The Process

Now that you understand how important values are for finding integrity in your past decisions and giving you the confidence to make future ones, it's time for you to discover your own values and turn these into a powerful statement that will motivate you. The process of identifying your values can be a hugely uplifting and powerful one. You will not only have a better understanding of what matters to you but also be able to articulate this in a way that makes it easy and practical to reference as you go forward. As with each stage of your Imposter Speech process, you can work through the below tasks on your own at home, or with the help and accountability of a group through the Imposter Speech Programme (for details of my Imposter programme go to **www.carolineflanagan.com/join)**.

In either case, be sure to download your free Imposter sheet to help you work through the process. (You can download your sheet here: **www.carolineflanagan.com/imposterspeech**).

TASKS

1. Desert island values

Imagine you have been told you are being evacuated to a remote island to start a new life. You get to take one suitcase, and in that suitcase you can only bring what you need to build a happy, successful, fulfilling life. The train leaves in five minutes, what do you take?

The aim of this challenge is to get you to think about what matters most to you and what values you couldn't live without. To help you decide this, consider the following questions. What do they reveal about what makes you feel happy and/or fulfilled? Don't limit yourself to a work situation. Think about your life in general.

- When was I most happy or excited?

- When was I most sad or devastated? (Your value will be the opposite of this)

- What's the first great thing that happened to me and what made it great?

- What's the most recent great thing I've experienced and why?

- When was the last time I felt good about myself and what was I doing?

- When was I most surprised? Thrilled? Disappointed?

- What am I most proud of and why?

- When have I been the most angry and upset?

For example, here are some of the answers I would give to these questions:

- Most happy: winning prizes; getting into Cambridge; travelling to Australia age 19; five offers of training contracts; publishing my first book; getting married; having each of my children.

- Most sad or devastated: being evicted; coming home to find all of my possessions were gone; witnessing a violent assault.

- Recent great thing: going on safari in South Africa.

- Most proud: running half-marathon, writing book.

2. Name that value

Once you have a list of experiences for reference, the next step is to identify the underlying value behind each experience. Ask yourself: what does this experience teach me about what matters to me?

If you get stuck, you can refer to the list of values in the Appendix as reference (you can also download a copy of this list on the website at **www.carolineflanagan.com/**

imposterspeech). Just be mindful to match the values to your actual experience. Don't be tempted to just select the values that you think you should have or would sound good to others!

VALUES

The following is a list of words or phrases that illustrate values. As you contemplate this list remember that it is not the word itself that is important so much as the meaning that you attribute to it. You may even feel that combining two or three values together brings you closer to the real feeling of a value and what it means for you.

Adventure	Growth
Beauty	Balance
Being authentic	Achievement
Excellence	Spirituality
Excitement	Zest
Freedom	Health
Friendship	Performance
Fun	Order
Honesty	Risk Taking

Humour	Loyalty
Love	Challenge
Nurturing	Tolerance
Openness	Autonomy
Recognition	Independence
Trust	Originality
Balance	Flexibility
Choice	Respect
Appreciation	Safety
Security	Stability
Reward	Care

Example: based on my experiences summarised above, I'd identify the following values:

- Safari in South Africa: adventure.

- Winning prizes, Cambridge etc: recognition, achievement, learning and growth.

- Getting married, having the boys: love, nurture.

- Eviction: security, financial independence.

- Marathon: challenge; fitness.

3. Going deeper

What does each word mean to you? It's great to have the specific word as an identifier of what's important to you, but the exercise is not complete until you've got really clear on what specifically each value means to you. Different values have different meanings for different people. My version of challenge or adventure may be different to yours. The clearer you are about this, the more powerful your values are going to be as a compass for decisions you make going forward and for your Imposter Speech.

For example:

VALUE: GROWTH

Meaning: I am continuously learning and evolving

VALUE: CHALLENGE

Meaning: I'm setting and achieving goals that seem impossible, defying the odds

Work through the values you've arrived at or selected. What is the significance of each value to you personally? What does it represent? Try to write a full description for each so that you are really clear about what each signifies.

Why am I here? – The Speech

Now you've completed the process, you know what motivates you and what you can use to drive your decisions. It's now time to convert this into a powerful motivational statement (or statements) that validates why you are here and can act as a compass going forward. You'll then add this statement to your Imposter Speech. Here are some different ways you can start your statement:

I'm here because…

What matters most to me…

What I care deeply about is…

What drives me is…

I'm passionate about…

I come alive when I…

I am at my best and happiest when I am…

You can use all or any combination of the above. Play around and test things out. Here is how my speech looks at this stage. I have added the relevant values in brackets so you can see how it works. It's important to note that I've been crafting, iterating and using my speech for years. If this is the first time you are creating yours, remember that this is your speech for your eyes only. There is no one to judge you, and you won't win any bonus points by making it perfect! Way more important than how you construct it is the feeling it gives you when you say it.

"My name is Caroline Flanagan.

I am an ex-City lawyer who is now a transformational coach, inspirational speaker, twice an author and mother of four boys.

What matters most to me is feeling safe and secure (Security).

I am at my best and happiest when I am feeling loved and I am loving (Nurture), when I'm laughing and delighting (Fun) and when I'm having new experiences (Adventure).

What drives me is learning new things and how I grow and evolve as a result (Growth). I come alive when I'm winning battles, defying the odds and achieving my impossible (Achievement)."

As you'll see from my example above, you don't have to include a reference to every value. Just pick those that speak to you in this moment. Later, when you start to use your speech in real life, you can start to adapt your speech to include the elements that are going to have the most meaning for you in that particular moment.

Remember, if you're struggling with any of this, exploring your core values with a buddy, a coach or as part of a group coaching programme will make this exercise less daunting.

Summary

»   The third step of the Imposter Speech is *"Why am I here?"*

»   The answer to this question can be found by exploring your values.

»   Knowing your values helps with Imposter Syndrome because it stops you undermining past decisions or behaviours.

»   Knowing your values helps build a stronger identity because it reveals you as someone who lives by design and creates your own results, rather than one who relies on luck or accident.

»   Create the third statement in your Imposter Speech by exploring your past experiences, and identifying the key values that have driven your past behaviour.

HOW DID I GET HERE?

"Whether you come from a council estate or a country estate, your success will be determined by your own confidence and fortitude."

—MICHELLE OBAMA

In the last chapter, we looked at Step 3 of the Imposter Speech, *"Why am I here?"*, which gave you a deeper understanding of the values that have driven your past decisions and brought you to where you are. You identified your core values and learned that you can use these to make confident decisions and as a compass going forward to keep you on track.

By now your Imposter Speech is really taking shape. With each step of the speech, you've been building your confidence layer by layer. As a result of the deep exploratory work you've been doing, you can probably feel yourself changing. This work goes so much further than the quick fix of trying to tell yourself you'll be fine, or you do deserve to be here. By building your confidence layer by layer, you are creating a new empowered imposter identity that can battle systemic bias and self-doubt, and win.

What is the fourth step of the Imposter Speech?

Now let's look at Step 4 of the Imposter Speech: "*How did I get here?*" The answer lies in your backstory – what you've had to overcome and who you've had to be to make it this far. This step is about the resilience and resourcefulness you have developed as a result of past difficulties or failures. This is going to be one of your greatest assets going forward.

At the end of this chapter, you'll create a powerful statement that recalls you at your most resilient and resourceful, adding another layer of strength to your confidence and giving you easy access to these qualities going forward.

The objective of this chapter is for you to understand your backstory and gain a much deeper understanding of what it has taken to get where you are today. If a past experience produces negative feelings like shame or regret, exploring it as part of this exercise will help you to reframe that experience as a backstory that serves you.

Your backstory is how you stay connected to your past self, it's how you remember how far you've come and it's how you give yourself recognition for everything it took to get here. As a result of doing the work in this chapter, you will have a powerful resource of proven skills and experiences to draw upon when you face future challenges. Your backstory will also serve as a powerful stimulus for ongoing growth and continuing the journey to fulfil your potential.

How knowing how you got here helps with your Imposter Syndrome

A feature of your Imposter Syndrome, particularly as a person of colour, is the awareness of how different your journey has been to those around you, and the mistaken belief that this difference means you are less qualified or able than your peers. But the opposite is true. This difference is what speaks to your value. Your journey to where you are now has exposed you to a unique combination of influences, cultures, relationships, experiences, failures, opportunities – everything that's ever happened to you or around you. Who you are is a product of all of this, which is why reflecting on that journey and creating a backstory that reminds you of this value is so powerful. It shows you that, rather than working against you, the differences underlying your Imposter Syndrome can work for you.

Movie directors know the meaning of a backstory. Rarely does a movie start with where the hero is in the present and then proceed chronologically to the end. Some of the best movies start with action from the present, and then spend the entire movie telling the story of how our hero got here and the experiences and adventures that make him or her unique. By the time the story picks up in the present again, we are hugely invested in our hero's success because we know what it has taken to get here.

Why knowing your backstory helps build a stronger identity

Your backstory helps to build a stronger identity because it's where you'll find two qualities that you'll need in life's arena when you come face to face with systemic bias or self-doubt: resourcefulness and resilience. These are two qualities you already have. When you consider where you are (Step 2), it's hard to see how you could have come this far and achieved what you have without them. But there's a world of difference between having something useful and knowing where to find it when you need it! The work you do for Step 3 of the Imposter Speech helps to extract the valuable lessons and experiences of your past and put these at your fingertips so they are easily accessible when you need them (you'll see how this works in Chapter 15).

Giving birth is a great example of how a backstory works. You don't have to be a parent to know that going through labour and bringing a new person into the world is a big deal. If you haven't experienced it yourself, you're bound to have seen a messy, noisy, suspense-filled re-enactment on TV that comes pretty close to the real thing, so this example will still work for you.

I've given birth four times. That means I've grown a new human being in my abdomen on four separate occasions, and when the time was ripe I've somehow squeezed them out of an impossibly small part of my body. So you can believe me when I tell you that giving birth hurts. It is painful and exhausting and if ever there was a challenge designed to break your spirit and reduce you to a blubbering wreck and leave you begging for mercy, labour is it.

And yet, I've done it four times. And each time I've done it naturally without any form of pain relief[17]. I'm not looking for a medal (though if they offered me one, I'd gladly accept it!). The reason I'm sharing this with you is because I want you to know the power of a backstory.

When I fell pregnant with my first, Dylan, I had no idea what labour and childbirth would actually be like. Sure, I'd heard all the stories and knew enough to be pretty scared. I'd followed the advice of my sister-in-law, Catherine, and watched a couple of live births on the Birthing Channel[18], which left me pretty traumatised, but at least gave me some idea of what to expect. But nothing really prepares you for the experience first-hand. It was terrifying, exhausting, painful, debilitating. It took every ounce of courage and determination and strength and stamina I had; and when I felt utterly broken and convinced I couldn't go on, it demanded ten times more.

After facing such a punishing experience the first time, how was I able to sail through labour, not just one, not two, but three more times, knowing how challenging it would be, but fairly confident I could get through it without pain relief? The answer is because, when it came to giving birth, I had a backstory. In other words, I had processed the experience of giving birth the first time and formed it into a story about what I'd learned: not just about childbirth, but about myself. I learned, for example, that even if it feels like it at the time, pain doesn't last forever. I learned that there are some things you have control over and many more things you don't so at a certain point you have to let go. I learned that focusing on your breathing will get you through pretty much anything life throws at you, and that if the journey feels too hard and long, it helps to stop thinking about the destination and just focus on putting one foot in front of the other; and I discovered that just when you think all is lost and you can't take it anymore, something amazing and surprising can happen.

I also learned about me. I learned that I am tough. I learned that when I feel broken and want to give up, there's something in me that will refuse to give up. I learned that I'm

You won't find your greatest strengths in the stories of your success; you'll find them in the stories of your failures.

not afraid to do hard things and that when I'm motivated to achieve a goal that's going to mean something (we talked about this in Step 3), I can get through anything. I learned that I'm resourceful, I'm resilient and I'm strong.

Can you imagine how different it was for me going into my second, third and fourth labours with this kind of back-story? With this kind of confidence in who I could be and what I could do and get through and accomplish? I wasn't born with that confidence, I created it by choosing to relive one of the most challenging experiences I've been through and by having the courtesy, curiosity and respect to ask myself: how did you do that? What does that say about you and what you are capable of? This is the power of your backstory. It's you telling you: you've got this; you've been tested and challenged before and you can do it again.

Some of my clients struggle with the backstory concept at first. They get the idea. After all, there's nothing ground-breaking about calling on a past experience and using it to inform what you're doing in the present. It's basically what you do every day in your work so you become more experienced and competent in a particular discipline or skill. But this is exactly the problem. My clients want to go looking for the answer in their successes, but they are looking in the wrong place. You won't find your greatest strengths in the stories of your success; you'll find them in the stories of your failures.

Which brings me to the second and perhaps most important reason your backstory is important: it forces you out of hiding. It forces you to look back on your journey to this point and shine the spotlight on the areas and in the corners and boxes and shelves where you don't want to go. This is where the pain and disappointments hide; the fears and the frustrations, the failures and the tragedies. These are the places none of us wants to go. But we need to because that's where the treasure is buried.

I know, because for years, this was me. I never wanted to dwell on the past. As soon as it was over, I was done with it. For years, all that mattered was where I was at that time and where I was going. I had good reason. As you've heard in Chapter 3, there was plenty in my past I wanted to forget. And besides, I was too busy battling the systemic bias and self-doubt in my present to have time to dwell on the past.

It was years before I discovered how the more challenging parts of my past could give me confidence in the future. I spent all those years thinking that the only valuable experiences were the highs: the times when I had won something or achieved something. I completely overlooked the value of the lows. The problem with this success-based approach to confidence is that it only works as long as you're winning and things are going your way. When everybody is cheering and supporting and including you and you feel valued. But life is an arena. The moments I'd spent collecting prizes and trophies were relatively limited. I'd spent most of the time face down in the dirt.

Step 4 of the Imposter Speech was for me the most challenging and transformative step of all. I realised that by hiding from my more challenging experiences, I was only showing up as half of me in my work and in my life, and that so much of my fear of taking risks and putting myself out there was built on the fear of how I'd got here. Creating my backstory was the hardest thing I've ever done and also one of the most powerful. I wouldn't be here, writing this book for you, if it weren't for my backstory. I wouldn't be showing up the way I do in my business and in my life if it wasn't for my backstory. What once felt like a source of weakness for me has become one of my greatest sources of strength. My backstory is what reminds me I'm unique and it's what makes me powerful and strong. In this step, I want to help you discover what your backstory can do for you.

IMPOSTER TRUTH

Most people, when they consider their past, focus on the mistakes, failures and difficulties they encountered. They have no idea that the real story of their past is not what they have been through, but how they were able to survive it.

So, how did you get here?

When you know your backstory, you get to understand what you are really made of. You get a glimpse of how strong and resilient you can be. Previously, the fear of failure and exposure that comes from your Imposter Syndrome would often hold you hostage, forcing you to play it safe and play small. But once you have your backstory, that fear can no longer hold you. It doesn't go away. As long as you are showing up and pushing to achieve your potential, it will continue. But because you recall what you've been through and you've connected with qualities and strengths you perhaps hadn't realised you had, you can step forward and take the risk. Before we get to the process of creating this part of the speech, what state is your backstory in now?

Do you overlook past failures and disappointments?

Fundamental to this step is your exploration of past failures and disappointments because the real power of how you got here won't be found in the moments when things went well for you or when you came out on top. Although these moments are important, they don't require nearly so much of you as the times when you failed, or felt like giving up (or did give up) or when life dealt you a blow. These are the moments when your strongest qualities show up, like courage, tenacity, grit and determination. So search back through your story and root out those failures and disappointments you've been overlooking. What I want you to discover is who you can be when you are in the thick of it and you need to fight your way out.

Do you avoid the dark corners?

Reflecting on failures and disappointments will get you some of the way there but this may not be enough. In order to release its powers, you need to mine your backstory for your deepest, darkest most challenging moments. These are the hard bits, the scariest bits, the darkest cobwebbed corners of your past where you refuse to go because of the pain and discomfort it may cause you. They are the moments of heavy disappointment, loss, hurt and anger. The times when you learned that life can be unfair and painful and mean. This may be the hardest thing I ask you to do, so I can understand it if you want to avoid this. If you have parts of your journey that have been particularly traumatic then obviously you should seek help and support going through this (from a qualified counsellor, for example) rather than take yourself to any vulnerable places alone. What I will say is that I successfully avoided these corners for years. But it wasn't until I was willing to go to all the dark corners of my journey that I experienced a true transformation.

Have you forgotten who you used to be?

A common mistake I see Imposter Syndrome sufferers make is being so caught up in who they are now, they lose sight of who they used to be and the road they have travelled to get here. It's not that you aren't connected to where you have come from, it's that you underestimate, undervalue or may even have forgotten what has happened in between.

This compounds your Imposter Syndrome. With little understanding of how you have evolved over time, you'll struggle to align a perception of who you were with the reality of who you are now.

Are you stuck in who you used to be?

This shows up in many people of colour who have fallen into the Authenticity Trap. Your sense of identity is fixed to a moment, memory or experience of the past, with no real appreciation of the new skills, lessons and behaviours you have amassed and adopted along the way. As a result, any action or suggestion that requires you to grow or adapt is seen as a strident threat to your sense of self. What this does is keep you stuck in time, and again prevents you from seeing the trajectory of your life and how you have evolved as a person over time.

How have you spun your backstory?

What stories are you telling yourself about your past? We all have a story about our past (you've read many of mine here) and because we have imperfect memories and our experiences of the past are highly subjective, we infuse that story with our own choice of meaning. Some people choose a backstory that is negative and depressing and paints them as a victim. Meanwhile, someone else could have those exact same facts in their backstory and paint a positive inspiring story with themselves as a hero. The facts are the same. It's just the positioning that is different.

Take my story, for example. I could have taken the very same facts of my life that I shared in Chapter 3 and created a negative story which painted me as the victim of a difficult childhood. But that backstory doesn't serve me, and the facts, when I look at them, point just as easily to a better, more empowered backstory, which is the one I consciously adopted for myself and chose to share with you.

How you tell and relive your story has a powerful impact on how you manage your Imposter Syndrome and on how your Imposter Speech serves you going forward. So when you explore your journey to this point, choose a backstory that serves and empowers you, not one that paints you as a powerless victim or brings you down.

How did you get here? – The Process

The journey you'll take in this step is a journey into your past experiences, with a particular focus on the failures and challenges you have encountered on the way. Imagine you're a gladiator who has been in the arena all day and at the end of the day you join a close group of fellow gladiators that you know and trust, and you tell them about your experience, especially the parts you found most challenging; where you wanted to give up. Now grab your Imposter Speech sheet (if you haven't already, go to **carolineflanagan.com/imposterspeech** to download this for free) and work through the following steps:

TASKS

1. 100 fails

Take a piece of paper and brainstorm your most challenging experiences. Challenge yourself to come up with at least 100. Because of our tendency to remember our failures over our successes, you may find this easier than coming up with 100 successes, which you did in Step 2! You may still find it hard to get to 100 fails, but again, that's the point. I want to get you thinking beyond the experiences of recent years and those that come immediately to the mind when you think of the past. Think more deeply, delve further. Here are some questions I use in workshops to jog people's memories:

- What are the major milestones in your life that stand out as failures?

- What would you consider your biggest failure?

- When were you most afraid?

- Think of a time when you almost gave up. What stopped you?

- Think of a time when you struggled the most. What did you do?

- If you could take one quality into battle, what would it be?

- What are your three most difficult memories?

2. Process your experiences

Look through your stories and choose those that are most evocative or powerful. Now you want to reflect on those stories and how they make you feel. What do they trigger and what did you learn from them that can serve you going forward. More questions to help:

- What does your backstory say about you?

- What have you had to do to survive, overcome and triumph?

- Who have you had to be?

- Find the words to describe the qualities you exhibited

- What have you learned about yourself?

- What did you learn about life from this experience?

3. Choose a defining moment

Reflect on your answers to the steps above, and pick out the defining moments – the more challenging the better. Then extract from these the resources and qualities it took to make it through or bounce back. If you have more than one defining moment, just go with the one that resonates most deeply today. You can always come back to another moment if you decide to adapt your speech at a later date.

I use my "revelation in a box" moment for this – the one where I opened the parcel from HM Prison Services, thinking it contained sweets and goodies and gifts, while my friends sat around and watched. From that experience and what it took to bounce back from that, I extracted courage, determination, grit, inner strength, persistence, focus and creativity. As you can see, there's no limit to the number of qualities you choose!

How did you get here? – The Speech

Now take the experience of your defining moment and use it to create the next layer of your Imposter Speech. Remember, your Imposter Speech is for you and you only, so there's nothing to hide. The more honest and authentic you can make it, the more powerful it will be for you, so don't hold back at this stage. It's fine to extend your "*How did I get here?*" statement over a few sentences. Here is a structure to help you do this. I've also included an example from my own speech below:

It has taken... [list qualities] *... to come this far.*

I've had to be...........

I've had to do...........

There was a time when........

But/In the end I........

My name is Caroline Flanagan.

I am an ex-City lawyer who is now a
transformational coach, inspirational speaker,
twice an author and mother of four boys.

What matters most to me is feeling safe and
secure (Security). I am at my best and happiest
when I am feeling loved and I am loving (Nurture),
when I'm laughing and delighting (Fun) and when
I'm having new experiences (Adventure).

What drives me is learning new things and how I
grow and evolve as a result (Growth). I come alive
when I'm winning battles, defying the odds and
achieving my impossible (Achievement).

It's taken grit and determination to get this far. I've had to be strong. I've had to be resilient and I've needed to think on my feet. It's also taken an unbelievable amount of courage. There were so many times when I wanted to give up, but each time I persevered. I put one foot in front of the other and I just kept going.

It takes work and time to reflect and a bit of trial and error to find the lines that speak to you. You may find yourself becoming quite emotional when you do this. Don't worry, it's all part of the process. You'll be revisiting experiences you may not have thought about in years, or which you've only ever thought about negatively, and discovering for perhaps the first time the amazing qualities they reveal about you. Doing this exercise with a partner or as part of a group will make this step significantly easier.

Summary

» The fourth step of the Imposter Speech is *"How did I get here?"*

» The answer to this question can be found by exploring your backstory.

» Your backstory is what you've had to overcome and who you've had to be to make it this far.

» Knowing your backstory builds a stronger identity because it's where you'll find evidence of your resourcefulness and resilience.

» Create the fourth statement of your Imposter Speech by choosing a defining moment and extracting the qualities and resources you used to get through it.

CHAPTER 14

WHERE AM I GOING?

*"Bringing the gifts that my ancestors gave, I am
the dream and the hope of the slave.
I rise. I rise. I rise."*

—MAYA ANGELOU

n the previous chapter, we looked at step 4 of the Imposter Speech, *"How did I get here?"* which explored who you have had to be and what you have had to do to get where you are today. You explored your backstory, learned how past difficulties and failures contribute to future confidence, and added a powerful resilience statement to your speech.

You're almost there. The layers of your confidence are building, compounding, strengthening. If you've done the work of the previous 4 steps you'll be starting to feel the difference. You'll be absorbing and assimilating the power in each of these statements. Taken together, they compound into something so much greater than the sum of their parts. We are not interested in glossing over the cracks. We're getting deep into the crevices and building from the ground up. One more step and your Imposter Speech will be complete and ready for use in the real world.

What is the fifth step of the Imposter Speech?

In this, the final step of the Imposter Speech, we are asking: "*Where am I going?*" The answer to this question can be found by getting clear on your purpose – in other words, what it is you want to achieve in the long-term – and ensuring that the short and medium-term goals you are chasing are aligned. At the end of this chapter, you'll create a powerful affirmation in the present tense, that will inspire you to fulfil your potential and give meaning to the struggles you will encounter along the way. You'll add this affirmation to your earlier statements to complete your speech, at which point you will be ready to start practising it in full and internalising its powerful message.

At the end of this chapter, you'll create a statement that ignites your sense of purpose so that you push through the struggle and persevere towards your goal. This is the statement that will complete your speech and channel the momentum you've built through steps one to four and give you the courage and confidence to take action.

Of all the steps in your Imposter Speech, this, for me, is the one that I find most motivating and inspiring. If the first four steps are about building solid ground, this step is about what you now have the power to do when you're standing on that solid ground. When you use the present tense to talk about a goal you want to achieve in the future and a wider purpose you want to serve, the effect is so powerful, it is almost eerie. You can almost feel the cogs of the universe shifting and aligning themselves around you to help you achieve the goals that will take you there. This is the power of affirmations. If you're sceptical about this sort of thing, I want you to trust me. You've come this far. This is the final magical piece in the puzzle that's going to give you the new imposter identity that will help you win your battles. As a result of completing this step, you will have clarity about what you are here to do and where you want to go. In other words, you will have found your purpose.

The aim of this final step of the Imposter Speech is to get you thinking about your goals and ambitions and what, in the long term, you want to achieve. I expect you already know all about the importance of goal-setting. But if you're anything like my clients, you don't spend nearly enough time actually fleshing out those goals and, even if you do, you give little thought to tying them to your wider purpose. Most likely, you haven't considered your purpose at all. This step aims to change that. As a result of doing this work, you'll have a deeper understanding of why your goals are worth pursuing and, thanks to your purpose, the motivation to persist through the challenges you encounter on your way to achieving them.

How knowing where you are going helps with your Imposter Syndrome

A key trait with Imposter Syndrome is being driven by the fear of exposure and doing everything you can to avoid it. You need *"Where am I going?"* to direct your attention away from what you are trying to avoid, namely exposure and fear, and towards what you want to achieve moving forward. Focusing on what we want to move towards is more powerful, effective and produces better results. You gain this from having achieved success, particularly where that success is connected to a higher purpose.

Why knowing your purpose helps build a stronger identity

Knowing your purpose builds a stronger identity because it helps you engage with your goals at a deeper level and gives meaning to the struggle you may face as you try to achieve them. The reason this achieves that is because it stops it being only about you. Whereas a goal tends to be for you (e.g. you want to be promoted), a purpose tends

"

When you have a goal and a purpose, doing the work and overcoming the challenges is not only easier, it's rewarding.

"

to be for a greater good (you want to be a role model to people like you, who want to be promoted).

A struggle with meaning is a completely different experience to a struggle that is merely attached to a goal. You're more invested in it. That's why people who have a purpose describe themselves as having a passion, being on a mission or having a dream. Their purpose is strong enough to outlive any struggle. One of the most inspiring examples of this is Martin Luther King's dream for racial equality and freedom. When he stood on the steps of the Lincoln Memorial in Washington on August 28, 1963, in front of a crowd of over 250,000 civil rights supporters, he didn't talk about his goals, he talked about his dream. This is what captured the hearts of the crowd and gave meaning to the suffering and sacrifices that were a feature of the Civil Rights Movement long after King's death.

You may want to have different purposes for different areas of your life. For example, I have a specific purpose for my family. At the time of writing, we're still in the midst of the global COVID-19 pandemic. So if this is still the case when you're reading this book, holidays may or may not be top of your list right now. But if you're anything like me, now that the temperatures are dropping and the autumn and winter months are fast approaching, dreaming about my next holiday is never far from my mind.

There is a reason for this, and it is the perfect illustration of how goals and purpose work and why they are important. At the time of writing, I'm dreaming of going to the Maldives at Christmas. You may think this is decadent (it is) and extravagant (most definitely). You may consider it naïve or overly optimistic. But at the end of last year (in the halcyon days before COVID), I had an extremely challenging Christmas, when I was worried I might lose my family. To help get us through this experience, I set the goal of spending Christmas 2020 on a beautiful island in paradise. I wanted us to experience Christmas somewhere magical. Somewhere we could spend quality time as a family where we could be outdoors, close to nature, doing lots of activities together and seeing and experiencing a beautiful part of the world – the food, the drink, the culture, the scenery.

What I've just described is a goal and a purpose for my family this year. The goal is to go to the Maldives. The purpose is to have an unforgettable experience that creates lasting family memories and fosters a closer connection between us.

But booking a holiday is not just about the destination (the goal). Neither is it only about the experience when you get there (the purpose). It's about everything that happens in the lead up to it. Sure, there's the excitement and looking forward to it, and the milestones you pass along the way to it. But there are also hurdles to overcome and challenges to be met: meeting deadlines; trying to hand off work for others to look after in your absence; saving the money; the logistics of travel; organising the kids; the packing and washing and sorting; even the holiday shopping can be rushed and stressful. I know you're familiar with the feeling when you're preparing to take time off and you realise that, by deciding to take time out from the pressures and stresses of a busy life, you have actually created more stress and pressure, and you've ended up with a longer to-do list and a shorter time to do it! But none of this matters to me. I'm prepared to put up with all of this. Why? Because the upfront struggle has meaning: when I get through it, I get to spend Christmas in the Maldives (my goal) and have an unforgettable holiday with my family (the purpose).

This is how your goals and purpose work in each area of your life. When they are real and compelling enough, they get you through the hard stuff. They give you something to get excited and enthusiastic about when the things you have to do to achieve it are tedious or difficult or scary. And there's more. Because you are more invested in it, that investment starts to become its own reward. When you have a goal and a purpose, doing the work and overcoming the challenges is not only easier, it's rewarding.

And yet, if you're anything like my clients, you spend little time on your goals. Even for the areas in your life where you may think you have goals, these are typically too vague or too "out there" – meaning, you're not connected to them at all. And when it comes to your purpose, my guess is that you have little idea at all.

I am calling you out on this because I know all about it. This used to be me. Don't get me wrong, I've always been very goal-driven. But what drove my goals was always what I wanted to get away from or avoid. I wanted to get away from worrying about money or ever being evicted and made homeless again, so I worked hard for a career that I knew would give me financial security (you'll recognise this as one of my values). I wanted to avoid being disrespected, judged or taken advantage of, so I chose a career that would give me recognition and respect. When I became a lawyer, I knew I wanted to eventually be a partner, but that was it, and it wasn't enough. The goal to "be a partner" was way too vague and too far removed. I didn't think about what sort of partner it was my goal to be, or what being a partner would look like or feel like.

Likewise, I hadn't connected my goal to an underlying purpose. OK, so I wanted to be a partner, but why and so what? What would this mean to me? What was it about the prospect of being a partner that I felt passionate about? What excited me? What would sustain my enthu-

347

siasm when the work was exhausting, the clients over-demanding and during those inevitable moments when I was afraid I might fail?

It took me years to discover the importance of having a positive goal and an underlying purpose. Years after I left my law career and started a coaching business, my Imposter Syndrome was still holding me hostage. I continued to set goals that were vague and distant – goals like "build a successful business" and "get more work-life balance" (everybody likes the latter one!). And I struggled in vain to align them to a purpose that was strong enough to get me excited. I have always worked hard. Extremely hard. I've always been driven. But I worked hard from a place of fear, and was driven by need. The fear of being found out and the need to prove I could succeed. My Imposter Syndrome had as strong a hold over me after I had left my high-flying legal career behind and become my own boss, as it had when I was in the thick of it.

But all that changed when I created my Imposter Speech. I started to use Step 5 to get really clear on the goals I wanted to achieve in different areas of my life, and then I'd peel back the layers of the goal until I found an underlying purpose that I could feel passionate and excited about. Not just a goal to get fit, but a goal to train three hours a week so I can keep up with my four extremely active boys; not just a goal to read more, but a goal to read one book a week so I can keep discovering ways to serve my clients better; not just the goal to grow my business but the goal to write this book so that I can use my experience and expertise to empower more people of colour to go out and fulfil their potential. The list goes on. And these goals get bigger and more ambitious because when the struggle has meaning, achieving the goal itself is only half the point. The journey towards the goal, what it asks of you along the way and who you become as a result, can be an even greater gift than achieving the goal itself.

This is the experience I want for you, and the reason why it's so important is because the path to success is never linear, it rarely happens the exact way you expect it and it almost always takes longer than you think! So in order to succeed, you must set goals which have an underlying purpose to them, and then step out into the arena and try to achieve them, knowing from the start that it won't always be easy. But the good news is you'll have Step 5 of your Imposter Speech to keep you motivated, inspire you to stay the distance and reward you with satisfaction and fulfilment along the way, instead of having everything riding on the end result.

"Where am I going?" is essentially about fulfilling your potential because fulfilling your potential isn't an end-point, it's ongoing, infinite. The point is not to be able to say you've done it, it's to be able to say you are doing it. That means the real value behind your goal and purpose lies in the journey you take to get there. To focus on the destination is to miss the point. It's not what happens when you get there, it's who you are becoming along the way. We'll talk more about this in the next chapter. But first, let's talk about where you are now in relation to your goals and purpose.

IMPOSTER TRUTH

People with Imposter Syndrome spend little, if any, time setting clear goals and it has never occurred to them to align these goals to a greater purpose.

So, where are you going?

Are you clueless about your purpose?

Most people haven't given much thought to their purpose, so if this is you then don't worry, you're not alone (and you're in the right place!). It's much more common to react and improvise your way through life, following the well-trodden path to achievement. It's a great way of clocking up achievements, but as we've seen, the struggle is harder and you miss out on the fulfilment you get from pursuing a meaningful goal, long before you ever have the satisfaction of achieving it.

If you are new to the idea of having a purpose, *"Where am I going?"* is yet another opportunity to get to know yourself better. If you've ever asked yourself "what's the point?" or "why do I bother?", or found it difficult to set goals, then this could be a yearning to connect to a deeper purpose so you can be more intentional about both how you live and with the results you want to create. This is exactly what Step 5 will help you do.

Does it feel like a struggle?

Think of a goal which you are trying to achieve right now that has presented a few challenges. Does it feel like a struggle? Perhaps you've received a "no" in response to a request for help or support in achieving your goal; or maybe the rejection is related to the goal itself: you're not going to be promoted this year, or you didn't get the new job, for example. If things aren't quite working out the way you'd like them to, and it's all starting to feel too much like hard work, ask yourself what the underlying purpose of your goal is. If you know the answer, this should give you the boost you need to keep going. You can keep your eyes on this prize (your purpose) and keep going. But without a purpose, it's hard not to be debilitated every time you experience a setback, and the prospect of facing more hurdles in the future can start to feel unbearable.

Are you in a hurry to succeed?

Almost without exception, all of my clients are in a hurry to achieve their goals and, unless I consciously remind myself, I'm the same! Is this you? Are you in a hurry too? Being ambitious and hard-working makes us hungry for results. At a certain point, we can't help thinking "surely I've done enough" and "I've worked so hard for this" or even, "this has taken far too long, when will it (the journey, the process, the exhausting pursuit) end?". (A certain someone may have had thoughts like this during the most challenging moments of writing this book!) We think the path to success should be proportionate to the effort invested and the desire behind it, and the time it takes to achieve our goal should be reasonable, even though this rarely reflects the reality. It doesn't help that we live in a world which taunts us, via social media, with images of instant success and gratification.

The problem with being in a hurry to succeed is that it makes the journey so much more difficult. The frustration it creates also increases the likelihood of you wanting to give up before you succeed, and the corners you might be tempted to cut in order to get there could end up setting you back further. If you are in a hurry to achieve your goals, focusing on your purpose will tame the frustration and anger that is triggered when things don't materialise the way we want or expect them to. Purpose helps you stay calm and keeps you grounded, and prepares you for the reality of how long things *really* take.

Do you have an upper limit?

Have you ever been on the brink of a big success and found yourself doing something to deliberately sabotage yourself? Has it ever occurred to you that you might be afraid of success? As Imposter Syndrome sufferers, we are used to acknowledging our fear of failure (to ourself at least), but we're not always aware of our fear of success. But when you remember that success usually makes our Imposter Syndrome worse rather than better (we talked about this unique feature in Chapter 2), it's logical that we would fear this too. Of course, as a high achiever, it's normal for you to push yourself to achieve a certain level of success. The problem occurs when there's a point beyond which you don't dare to go, even though those around you see you have the potential to exceed it. Writer Gay Hendricks, author of *The Big Leap*, calls this our upper limit — an automatic ceiling or cut-off point (the result of our life experiences and influences) which kicks in whenever we are in danger of going beyond a certain level of success. The result is that you unconsciously sabotage your own success as a way of ensuring you don't exceed the limit.

You know that feeling when the idea of success terrifies you? That's your upper limit at work. It's trying to keep you small and in the zone where you feel most comfortable.

"Where am I going?" helps you to raise your upper limit by bringing the power of your long-term purpose to now. It can be so much easier to push through our self-imposed limitations and take a risk when you know that it's for the benefit of others.

Do you lack focus?

But *"Where am I going?"* isn't only about the lofty intangible of your purpose and vision. It's also about where you are trying to get to right now. This is the goal-setting element. It creates an essential focal point towards which you can direct the power of your Imposter Speech in the exact moments when you need it the most: during an interview or at the beginning of a speech; before an exam; during an important meeting and of course when you're battling systemic bias. Or even just to motivate yourself out of bed on a day when you'd rather be hiding from the world.

As a high potential person of colour, I expect you are very goal-oriented. How else could you have come this far? If this is you, then you may already have a list of goals you are pursuing in your life and career right now, which is great news. For you, the danger is that you either have too many goals (no constraint) or the goals you have set for yourself are way too vague (no clarity). Think of your goals as targets. Without constraint, there are too many targets to aim for. If you're trying to achieve too much at once, you'll become so thinly spread that however hard you work, you can only make a limited amount of progress towards each goal. Without clarity, the issue is you can't see the target. You know it's there somewhere and you're looking in the right direction, but most of your energy goes into trying to find it.

If you don't see yourself as naturally goal-oriented, revisit your 100 successes from the work you did in Step 2 (*"Where am I?"*). Most outcomes start off as ideas and then turn into decisions that drive actions that produce results (in this case, your successes). If you work back through this sequence (what action produced those results? What decisions or ideas led you to take those actions?) you may discover that your successes were more intentional than you think.

The key word when it comes to goals is focus. When you're aiming for something, make sure you put up a target that you can see clearly and then keep it in your sights.

Where am I going? – The Process

Now that you understand the importance of having a goal and an underlying purpose, it's time to identify yours. The key thing to remember about this part of the process is that it takes time. While you may be able to identify your goals quite quickly, you're unlikely to find your purpose within five minutes of sitting down to think about it. You're going to have to try things out and see what feels good. The good news is that by completing the previous steps of your Imposter Speech, you've really been getting to know yourself – what you are capable of achieving (Step 2: "*Where am I?*"), what drives you (Step 3: "*Why am I here?*") and the kind of stuff you're made of (Step 4: "*How did I get here?*"). Your sense of identity is so much stronger now and this is going to make finding your purpose so much easier.

Here are the tasks and questions that have helped me find my goals and purpose, which I walk through with my clients. Grab a piece of paper or your Imposter Speech worksheet (if you don't have a worksheet, go to **caroline-flanagan.com/imposterspeech** to download this for free) and let's begin:

TASKS

1. Map out your goals

For this first task, you can either use the free Imposter Speech download I've created for you (if you haven't already, you can download it here **carolineflanagan.com/ imposterspeech**) or draw your own goals map.

To draw your own, take an A4 piece of paper (turn it sideways so it is landscape), draw a circle in the middle and write the word "Goals" inside the circle. Now draw eight even spaced lines from the centre circle towards the edges of the paper. Your drawing should look like a spider. If all of this sounds like too much hard work, why not use the download. On each line, write down one of your core values which you identified in step 3. These are the things that matter most to you. This will ensure that your goals hold some real value for you. This is why your values are the perfect pillars around which to structure your goals.

Once you have the basics of your map, it's time to start adding goals. For each of your values, brainstorm your goals for the next 12 months and then choose the three that you like the most right now. Now draw three short lines from each of your main spider legs (as if those legs had fingers on the end), and at the end of (or just above) each of those lines, write down your three chosen goals. Repeat this for each core value.

Here are four of my values and corresponding goals for the next 12 months (to see the full list and goal map, head over to **carolineflanagan.com/imposterspeech**). I've used X and Y to avoid distracting you with my numbers! When you are deciding on your goals, be sure to include specific numbers in your list for clarity and focus.

Core value: Achievement – it's all about the book this coming year!

- *Be the bestselling author of Be The First*
- *Launch the Imposter Speech Coaching Programme*
- *Deliver a live Be The First keynote on a big stage*

Security/ Financial independence:

- *Double business revenue*
- *Reduce mortgage by X*
- *Increase savings by Y*

Core value: Adventure

- *Go snorkelling in the Maldives*

- *To go skiing again!*

- *To have a long weekend in Berlin*

Health/fitness:

- *Attend a fitness camp with my oldest son, Dylan*

- *Do 50 burpees in a row – and enjoy them*

- *Cook at least 10 recipes from the Body Camp Food Bible*

There's no magic to picking goals. The best advice, if you get stuck, is to look around you for inspiration. Get ideas from the news, social media and people you know or read about, but be sure to choose ones that truly appeal to you. My amazing neighbour Anne took up open water swimming in her fifties. She is just incredible. I admire her enormously, but there is absolutely nothing about open water swimming that appeals to me. Actually, that is a complete understatement. I have such a dislike of being cold, let alone cold and wet, that even the words themselves – "open water" – send an icy shiver down my spine. Not me. No thanks.

So pick something that does speak to you, and gets your heart thumping with excitement, even if some of that thumping is down to fear. The last rule is that you should be as specific as possible. Don't just say you want to go on holiday, say where. Don't just write down "get fit", write down the things you want to do or achieve as a result of being fit (run a marathon, for example).

2. Find your purpose

Once you have your goals, the next step is to find your underlying purpose. To do this, I recommend you pick one goal that is front of mind for you right now. Now, to find your underlying purpose, work through the following purpose questions:

- If I achieve this goal, what will it mean?

- When I achieve this goal, how will it impact others?

- When I achieve this goal, what will it say about me?

- When I achieve this goal,

   ...how might the people I love be different?

   ...how might the people I know be different?

   ...how might the world be different?

I appreciate that these are tough questions to read on a page in a book without the live prompting and support of a coach. I'm asking you to go big and imagine that you could make a difference in the world around you, something you may never have considered before. To help make things easier, here's an example.

GOAL: WRITING A BESTSELLING BOOK

If I achieve this goal, what will it mean?

I will have brought something valuable, useful and unique into the world.

When I achieve this goal, how will it impact others?

It will empower them to overcome barriers to success and inspire them to fulfil their potential.

When I achieve this goal, what will it say about me?

I am an example of what is possible when you use the Imposter Speech to turn your Imposter Syndrome from a weakness into a strength.

When I achieve this goal,

…how might the people I love be different?

They will be proud.

...how might the people I know be different?

They will be inspired.

...how might the world be different?

More people of colour will be inspired and empowered to progress their career and bring more diversity, inclusion and equality into leadership.

When I answer those questions, can you see the difference it makes to my goal? Now imagine what a difference it made, during the more challenging times of writing this book, to remember that it's not really about me. It's about an important message, with the potential to impact people I have never even met, and to contribute to the battle for racial equality. When a goal has this kind of meaning, the struggle is not only worth enduring, it also makes sense because the effort required feels proportionate to the desired result.

Now, I know what you're thinking. You're thinking that this exercise is easier to do if you're doing something like writing a book because, by design, its whole purpose is to inspire and empower other people. So in answer to that, and to show that any goal can have a purpose, here's the same exercise done with my burpees goal:

GOAL: 50 BURPEES IN A ROW

If I achieve this goal, what will it mean?

I am pretty fit!

When I achieve this goal, how will it impact others?

They'll see that it's possible to do burpees and enjoy them.

When I achieve this goal, what will it say about me?

I like a challenge, I'm committed and determined and I'm someone who will work hard to get the result I'm seeking.

When I achieve this goal,

...how might the people I love be different?

There'll think I'm mad but they'll be impressed!

...how might the people I know be different?

They'll be curious to find out whether burpees are something they could grow to love.

...how might the world be different?

Burpees may go from being the exercise people love to hate, to being the exercise of choice for staying fit and healthy.

Now imagine what it would be like for me doing those burpees with this kind of mindset. Imagine how many times I'm going to keep trying, and how much progress I'm going to make each time I practise when I have it in my head that my burpees could change the world! It may sound like a ridiculous example, but it just goes to show how any goal can have a purpose, and the difference that purpose makes to achieving a goal. Now let's move on and create the last line of your speech.

Where am I going? – The Speech

Once you have the answers to your purpose questions, it's time to convert this into an inspiring statement to add to the other lines of your speech. To do this, refer back to your answers to the exercises above and, choosing one goal only, use your answers to complete the following sentences:

My goal is to... [insert one goal]

And now here I am... [insert purpose] – this must be in the present tense. See the example from my speech opposite.

My name is Caroline Flanagan.

I'm an ex-City lawyer who is now a transformational coach, keynote speaker, twice an author and mother of four boys.

What matters most to me is feeling safe and secure (Security). I am at my best and happiest when I am feeling loved and I am loving (Nurture), when I'm laughing and delighting (Fun) and when I'm having new experiences (Adventure).

What drives me is learning new things and how I grow and evolve as a result (Growth). I come alive when I'm winning battles, defying the odds and achieving my impossible (Achievement).

It's taken grit and determination to get this far. I've had to be strong. I've had to be resilient and I've needed to think on my feet. It's also taken an unbelievable amount of courage. I've wanted to give up so many times, but each time I persevered. I put one foot in front of the other and I just kept going.

My goal is to publish a bestselling book on Imposter Syndrome for people of colour; and now here I am, inspiring and empowering people of colour around the world to become leaders of colour and help bring more diversity, inclusion and equality into leadership.

Or...

And now here I am, doing 50 burpees; and inspiring others to make burpees their exercise of choice for staying energised, fit and healthy.

As with all the steps of your Imposter Speech, you may find it helpful to work through your goals and purpose with a coach or as part of the Imposter Speech programme, where you can work with others in a small group.

Make the Imposter Speech yours

Congratulations on coming this far and creating your speech. I know it's been quite a journey and one that may have thrown up all sorts of feelings for you. If this is the case, you'll be pleased to know that the hard work is done. Everything you do from here will be about reinforcing the work you've already done and putting it all into practice.

In the next chapter, we're going to look at how you can start using your speech in all of those situations in the real world where your Imposter Syndrome shows up and threatens to hold you back or throw you off track. But before we do that, there's one last bit of work you need to do on your speech, and that is to internalise it and make it yours.

Now, of course, the speech is already yours in terms of ownership. You created it, and have poured yourself into it. But it's still new, so the chances are that you may be feeling unsure or awkward about it. Perhaps this is the first time you've ever attempted talking to yourself with such powerful intention. That's why you need to familiarise yourself with it. Think of it like a new pair of shoes that you need to try on, practise walking around in and get used to before you can really feel good in them. The more times you wear them, the more comfortable they feel and the more they adapt to the shape of your feet. We want to achieve exactly the same result with your Imposter Speech so that it starts to feel part of you.

Here's what you need to do to make your Imposter Speech your own:

- Write your speech down and leave it in places where you'll see it and read it every day.

- Say it out loud daily in front of the mirror until it becomes familiar enough for you to remember. If you make it something you do after brushing your teeth, it will easily become a habit.

- When you say it out loud, say it like you mean it – with energy and intention.

- If it feels uncomfortable at first, reassure yourself that you're doing it right.

- Take each section of the speech separately at first, focusing on just that section for a week and revisiting and saying it every day, before moving on to the next, so as not to be overwhelmed.

- Change, tweak and adapt your speech along the way as you practise saying it to ensure you are using the words and phrasing that work for you.

- Share your speech with a close friend, family member or even colleague that you trust, if you want their help to internalise the message. Ask if you can practise saying it out loud to them.

With the completion of Step 5, you have everything you need to step into the arena and start winning your battles. In the next chapter, I'm going to share some examples of how this works so you can start using it in the real world yourself.

Now that you've internalised your message, it's time to come and join me in the arena.

Summary

» The fifth step of the Imposter Speech is *"Where am I going?"*

» The answer to this question lies in knowing your goals and your purpose and making sure both are aligned.

» *"Where am I going?"* helps with Imposter Syndrome by switching your focus away from the negative consequences you are trying to avoid, like exposure and failure, to the positive things you want to achieve, such as specific goals and purpose.

» Knowing your purpose helps you engage with your goals at a deeper level and gives meaning to the struggle you may face as you try to achieve them.

» The real value behind your goal and purpose lies in the journey you take to get there.

» Create the closing line of your Imposter Speech by restating your name as you did in Step 1, and saying it with intention.

INTO THE ARENA

(USING YOUR IMPOSTER SPEECH IN THE REAL WORLD)

"It is not the critic who counts; not the man who points out how the strong man stumbles, or where the doer of deeds could have done them better. The credit belongs to the man who is actually in the arena, whose face is marred by dust and sweat and blood; who strives valiantly; who errs, who comes short again and again because there is no effort without error and shortcoming; but who does actually strive to do the deeds; who knows great enthusiasms, the great devotions; who spends himself in a worthy cause; who at the best knows in the end the triumph of high achievement, and who at the worst, if he fails, at least fails while daring greatly..."

THEODORE ROOSEVELT'S SPEECH
"CITIZENSHIP IN A REPUBLIC"

APRIL 23 1910, FRANCE

Part III was about the process and creation of your empowering Imposter Speech. Now you have your Imposter Speech, you're ready to start using it in the real world so you can be the first. But what does that mean? This book isn't just about creating a speech. It's about giving you a practical tool you can use in the real world that is going to make a difference to how you feel and what you do from this point on.

Now that you have the tool, I'm going to show you how you can use it. I'm going to share some examples of specific scenarios in which you might call on it. Some of these scenarios come straight from my own experience of using my Imposter Syndrome in real life, others are examples from clients I have coached who have experienced a transformation as a result of using this tool. I'm going to show you what the Imposter Speech has done for me and my imposter clients, so you can see what it can do for you.

As a result of reading this chapter, you'll really start to understand how powerful and practical this tool really is and you'll have the confidence to go out into the world and start using it right away.

Why you need the Imposter Speech in the real world

To be the first – to show up as an imposter and be committed and determined to succeed – is a great achievement but it isn't easy. Life is an arena. It's often challenging, at times it's unpredictable and it certainly isn't always fair. As a person of colour striving for success in a white world, you know this more than most. Sometimes you feel sure of what you're doing and where you're going, but more often than not you feel out of your depth and unsure of the next step. Some people help and support you, and then there are others who would rather prejudge or criticise or exclude you. And to complete this picture of uncertainty, there are no guarantees of success. How do you find your way in life's arena? How do you overcome the challenges, achieve success and know when you are fulfilling your potential?

I feel as though this is the question I've been asking myself my whole life, unconsciously at first, but with greater awareness since I started working with people with Imposter Syndrome. And the Imposter Speech has become my best answer.

To suffer from Imposter Syndrome is to fight an internal battle of self-doubt that threatens to hold you hostage in all those moments when you are about to, or have the opportunity to, fulfil more of your potential. As we saw in Chapter 2, to suffer from Imposter Syndrome when you're a person of colour trying to succeed in a white world is to fight a war on two fronts: the internal battle against self-doubt that holds you back and the external battle against inequality that keeps you down.

Enter your Imposter Speech – a powerful tool that switches your focus from that which makes you feel powerless outside of you to the power you have inside of you – to transcend barriers and achieve more than you believed was possible. Before we take a look at the specific scenarios in which you can achieve this, let's first take a look at how it works.

Guidelines for using your Imposter Speech

The Imposter Speech works. Use it correctly and repeat-edly and you will change. How you see yourself, how you act and how you approach the challenges you face in life's arena from this day forward – all of this will change. I know this because I have seen the effect it can have on others. And even more compellingly, I have experienced this change for myself. The fact that you are holding this book in your hand is testimony to that.

In order to get the full benefit of your speech's transfor-mational qualities, there are a number of guidelines you need to follow. These are:

Adapt it to fit your circumstances

How you use your Imposter Speech in the real world depends on the circumstances. There'll be times and circumstances when you need it to call you to action or get you through a mountain of fear, and you'll therefore need to recite the full speech. At other times, you may only need a reminder of who you are ("My name is..."), or of why you're choosing a course of action ("I am at my best when..."). The best way to work out what you need in any given moment is to try it and see what works.

Experiment

The Imposter Speech is a highly flexible tool. I'm going to share examples of scenarios in which you may want to use it, but this list isn't exhaustive. Likewise, how you use your Imposter Speech in each scenario isn't fixed. The way you would use it to get into the right state for an important meeting, for example, might be different to the way I would use it. The answer then, in all cases, is to experiment. There is no right or wrong way to use it, there's only the way that works for you. You may have to experiment and try it in different ways to discover that.

Use it or lose it

Your Imposter Speech isn't a simple tool that you can leave to gather dust in your toolkit, only bringing it out when you need it. It's a tool that requires care, maintenance and constant upgrading. And it needs to be used. It's not enough to create it. If you want it to work for you in real life, going forward, then use it. Practise using it in different scenarios to solve different problems. If you feel confident about others seeing it, print it out and have it on the wall near your desk so you see it every day, or share it with a trusted friend, colleague or family member directly.

Write it or speak it

When creating your Imposter Speech as part of the process outlined in Part III, the speaking part is key. It's really important that you hear it in your own voice and you say it repeatedly and with meaning. The experience of saying it out loud out can, at first, be an uncomfortable one. You might feel self-conscious and awkward. Some of my clients have felt embarrassed, even stupid, speaking to themselves like that in the mirror. All of the emotions and feelings that this self-confrontation brings up are important. As they change, as you feel more comfortable with your Imposter Speech, so do you.

However, once you are familiar with your Imposter Speech and are out using it in the real world, it's also useful to write it down. As you'll see below, you can use the speech as a step-by-step process to work through to help you solve problems or get unstuck. When you use it this way, it's important that you write down your responses as you work through each of the 5 steps. This gets them out of your brain and onto a place which allows you to get some distance from them and take a look at them, all to help you find a solution that will move you forward.

Benefits of using your Imposter Speech

When you have followed the correct process for creating your Imposter Speech, as outlined in this book, and you start using it in the real world, you're going to experience some really concrete results:

You build confidence in yourself over time

Having a deeper understanding of who you are, how far you've come and the qualities you've developed along the way will change the way you see yourself. Over time, with repeated use of your speech in the ways which I illustrate below, the way you see yourself will change.

You generate courage in the moment

In addition to helping you to build a deeper, longer-lasting confidence in yourself, the Imposter Speech also gives you courage in the moment. For all those times when you are either expected to take action or want to take action but you doubt yourself or are afraid of failure, the Imposter Speech is an instant courage boost. Because you've created and internalised it, you'll be able to recall the motivation, drive, purpose, and resourcefulness acquired over a lifetime of past successes, failures and life experiences, in the exact moment you need it.

You can coach yourself along the way

One of the joys of the Imposter Speech is the creation process. Not only is it a road map that takes you to a new empowered imposter identity; it is also a great coaching "model" (a series of questions to work through to coach yourself to a solution). Whatever issue you may be struggling with, you can work through the 5 steps of the speech creation process to give you clarity or get unstuck. See below for an example of how to do this.

Using the Imposter Speech in the real world

There is no limit to the ways you can use Imposter Syndrome to help you push through the fear and self-doubt, and to find your power in situations that would otherwise leave you feeling powerless. Below, you will find just some of the ways I use all or part of my Imposter Speech to serve as examples of when you can use all or part of yours too:

When introducing myself

I always use my full name to introduce myself. The most obvious context is in a professional setting – when meeting someone for the first time at a meeting or a networking event, for example. But I use it outside of work too. It's not my work persona, it's me, and so I use it everywhere. Recently I used it to introduce myself to the new postman who has just started doing the rounds in the town where I live. Meanwhile, I almost never answer a call from an unknown number with a "hello?", preferring instead to say "Caroline Flanagan". The caller knows immediately who they've called, which is helpful, of course, but the main reason I do it is because it's an easy way to stay connected to my Imposter Speech and practise summoning its power. Use *"Who am I?"* as often as you can to introduce yourself using your full name. Remember Bernadette Cooper who you met in Chapter 10? Say your name like you mean it, like it's something of value and loudly, clearly and slowly enough for those around you to hear it and be able to remember it.

When receiving negative feedback

I like to think of negative feedback as a gift (you can hear me talk about this in Episode 33 of The Caroline Flanagan Podcast – **www.carolineflanagan.com/episode33**), but it doesn't always feel like that when you receive it! I remember reviewing the feedback forms after one of my first keynote talks on Imposter Syndrome. Most of the feedback was overwhelmingly positive, but one comment was devastating. It said, "You're a fake and a fraud." I was mortified. I sat on the floor in the corner of my kitchen and cried and told myself I would never get on a stage ever again. Who was I kidding, thinking I had something to teach that others could benefit from. And when I finished crying I turned to my speech: *"Where am I?"* forced me to look and see that one comment in the context of everything else I had achieved; *"How did I get here?"* reminded me I was tougher than this; I'd been through worse and I'd come out the other side: and *"Where am I going?"* helped me to process the feedback constructively – how could that feedback help me to improve? It wasn't obvious at first, but I learned to understand that people have different ways of processing what they hear. I realised that it was unfair of me to "prefer" this one piece of negative feedback over those who had gained something from my talk. Oh, and lastly, I realised that as I went through the world reaching more people, not everyone would like me. And that's ok!

When I'm out of my comfort zone

As a person of colour with Imposter Syndrome, you'll be no stranger to the horrible feeling of being out of your comfort zone. Sometimes you have no choice, at other times you'll choose to leave your comfort zone because you want to grow and acquire new skills or experiences. The anxiety and stress this can cause as you teeter on the brink of what (to an Imposter Syndrome sufferer) can feel like the abyss of failure can be paralysing. I've had my fair share of these moments (delivering keynotes, pitching to a new corporate client, in the early days when I first started the podcast, delivering my first workshops etc.) and they haven't gone away just because I have my Imposter Speech (I guess if those moments stopped being uncomfortable, they'd no longer qualify as being out of my comfort zone!). Since creating my Imposter Speech, however, how I react to those moments has changed completely. I say the whole speech (sometimes to myself, at other times out loud, depending on where I am) to sum up all the courage and confidence I can, I take a deep breath and I go for it. The effect my Imposter Speech has is to cut out all the thought drama, which is all the negative thinking and criticism that your inner voice fills your brain with, leaving you too confused and terrified to act. (Have a listen to Episode 52 of the podcast to hear me talk more about thought drama – **www.carolineflanagan.com/episode52**). With its "this is who you are, what you've done, what matters, what you can do, where you're going" no-nonsense message, there's no room to dwell on my self-doubt. There's work to do.

When an opportunity presents itself

When an opportunity comes along that will be good for my business, but I'm unsure whether to seize it, I turn to my Imposter Speech. *"Why am I here?"* reminds me what matters most and helps me determine whether it will lead to something meaningful or fulfilling, while *"Where am I going?"* helps me distinguish between what will take me closer to my goals and purpose, and what is purely a distraction. I had an opportunity, recently, to deliver a talk at Middle Temple, a very prestigious barristers' chambers in London. Honestly, I was extremely busy at the time and the topic they had asked me to talk on was not on Imposter Syndrome, which was my singular focus at the time. I prepared to turn it down. But *"Why am I here?"* reminded me how important growth, challenge, achievement and recognition are to me. With the prospect of a global audience of barristers, judges and High Court judges, I realised that the opportunity ticked all of those boxes, and so I accepted.

When leading others

I use my Imposter Speech to help me be a more authentic leader. Previously, I would never have felt it appropriate to show any weaknesses or vulnerability. I thought being a leader meant getting everything right, doing everything perfectly and doing your best not to let others see when you fell short of those impossible standards. But all that did was create a distance between me and those I was supposed to lead. Now I am much more authentic when working with my team. I share *"Why am I here?"* so they understand the values that drive my decisions. I also give them glimpses of *"How did I get here?"* so they know that my achievements are hard-won and that I've had my share of setbacks and failures, and I use *"Where am I going?"* to help them see the bigger picture and get them on board.

When I feel I'm not enough

I have times when my Imposter Syndrome is acute and I tell myself I'm not enough of a long list of things I think everybody else is and I am spectacularly not. It happens less and less these days – a sign of the long-term transformative effects of my Imposter Speech (more about this below), but it happens. The end of 2019 was such a time. Life dealt me a killer blow. One of those blows that pulls the rug from under your feet, sucks the air out of your lungs and leaves you grasping desperately for a lifeline that isn't there. I tortured myself with that list of not-enoughs. I enveloped myself in it and wallowed in the pain and misery of it. I'll admit it to you: when I turned to my Imposter Speech, it felt hollow and fake. When I tried to say it aloud, the words tasted like ash in my mouth. *"Who am I?"* became a question I no longer knew how to answer. The Imposter Speech had its limitations after all.

Or at least, that's what I thought.

As it turned out, my Imposter Speech was working for me here too, delicately, surreptitiously. When I was consumed by despair and couldn't bring myself to turn to it, it sat there in a quiet corner of my mind and waited. And then in the early hours and the quiet moments, it would throw me a challenge:

"Who am I?"

"How did I get here?"

"Where am I going?"

These questions bobbed up and down on the surface of my mind continuously and there they sat, patiently, until finally, the answers floated up from deep within me to meet them.

"My name is Caroline Flanagan..."

I hope you don't experience many dark moments like these. But life is an arena, the conditions are never perfect and there are times when you may hit a wall. When this happens, a well-practised Imposter Speech can be a lifeline. It can ground you, steady you, keep you afloat, lift you – whichever form of support you need, this powerful tool can provide it.

When I'm setting goals

Your Imposter Speech is a great tool to use when setting goals. I love setting new year's resolutions, and never miss the opportunity to jumpstart a new year with fresh goals and new ambitions. If you're a goal-setter like me, you'll find your Imposter Speech an asset during these times. Ask yourself *"Why am I here?"* to ensure your goals align with your values and what matters most, and *"Where am I going?"* to remind yourself to connect your short-term goals with the long-term purpose you uncovered in

Chapter 13. Lastly, I find *"How did I get here?"* a useful way to prepare for the challenge of achieving a new goal – a reminder of all the resources I have at my disposal.

When I'm trying to be perfect

When you're caught up in the need to do everything perfectly (as Imposter Syndrome sufferers typically are), use your Imposter Speech. I have found it an invaluable tool for easing the pressure when I convince myself that nothing but perfection will do. It shifts my focus from the value of what I'm doing to the value of who I am. What this looks like in practice is me writing out or saying my speech in full and taking a look at it. The most powerful part of this process for me is *"Where are you going?"* because it reminds me that it's not about arriving at the destination, it's about the journey. And then I remember that when you pursue perfection there is no arrival. There can only be the journey towards it. So my objective shifts from a need to be perfect (or produce perfection), to a desire to be better (or produce something better) than before – an infinitely more attainable and rewarding objective.

When I'm stuck, I use the Imposter Speech as a coaching model

Sometimes you just get stuck. Maybe it's a decision you're struggling to make, or an opportunity you're unsure whether to go for. Or it could just be that you're feeling

385

down and despondent and going through one of those phases when it feels like nothing is working out. Whenever you're stuck, turn to your speech, only this time, use it as a coaching model. A coaching model is a series of questions you can work through which give you the clarity you need to move forward. Because your speech brings you back to the core essentials of who you are (where you are, why you're here etc.) it cuts through the confusion and creates a clear pathway for moving forward. I use it all the time. If I'm stuck on a decision, there's a problem I'm trying to solve or I feel I've lost my mojo, my Imposter Speech is where I turn. When I work through the steps of the speech, usually by writing out my answers in full, somehow it all becomes clear. If I am feeling despondent or low, my answers to *"How did I get here?"* and *"Where am I going?"*, give me a huge motivational boost. If I'm feeling anxious, it calms and steadies me. When I'm indecisive, the power of why I am here and where I am going seems to show me the way forward. But it's not an exact science. You never know which bit of the speech is going to work best, so always work through all the questions. Sometimes, it's the working through each layer that creates the shift.

Be prepared to change

The more you use your Imposter Speech, the better you'll become at drawing strength from it when you need it and adapting it to different circumstances. With consistent use, you may even start to embody it. In other words, instead of it feeling like a tool that you use, it will start to feel part of you.

I've been using my Imposter Speech for four years. I've said it and drawn strength from it so many times I'm no longer separate from it. The effect this has had on me has been gradual but dramatic. I'm changing. It feels like I'm gradually letting go but still holding on to what grounds me. When I'm in a challenging situation, I still experience the same feelings – the fear and anxiety, the urge at times to retreat back to safety – but it's as if I'm observing them because they don't have the same power over me anymore. After years of putting my Imposter Speech to practical use, it's so much a part of me that I no longer need to say the whole speech. I can look at myself in the bathroom mirror before a big talk, and say, "I am Caroline Flanagan", or I can let the words flash silently through my head when I'm in an important meeting – "I am Caroline Flanagan", and that's all it will take. I don't even have to say the whole speech. Before I know it, the fear melts away and all I'm left with, instead, is the courage to get to work. If you commit to making this tool work for you in the real world, this change could happen for you too.

Are you ready to start using your Imposter Speech in the real world? Can you imagine yourself using it in any of the scenarios above? If you're unsure where to start, just pick one and give it a try. Don't wait until your speech is perfect and don't wait for the "right" opportunity. Why not put this book down right now, go and stare in a mirror and give it a try?

If you're feeling some resistance to this that's natural and to be expected. Honestly, there have been times in the past where I've questioned whether a simple set of questions could do so much. There have also been times when I worry that it's so effective, it will get rid of my Imposter Syndrome altogether. Believe it or not, this scares me! I've been an imposter all my life and I wonder who I'll be if I no longer am one.

Everybody's Imposter Speech is different and everybody's experience of using it is different. I can't tell you exactly how it will work for you, but I can tell you that it will work if you create it and use it as I've shown. It is working for my imposter clients. It is working for me. It's time for the Imposter Speech to work for you.

Summary

» Use the Imposter Speech repeatedly and it will change you: how you see yourself, how you act and how you approach the challenges you face in life's arena will all change.

» Adapt your Imposter Speech to your circumstances and experiment with how and when you use it.

» It's important to speak your Imposter Speech so you get comfortable with hearing the words. However, there are certain scenarios when it is useful to write it down.

» You can use your Imposter Speech in a variety of ways, from coaching yourself to getting instant access to courage in the moment.

» In time, your Imposter Speech will stop feeling like a tool and start feeling like part of you.

» Don't wait until your speech is perfect and don't wait for the 'right' opportunity before you give it a try.

My name is Caroline Flanagan.

I'm an ex-City lawyer who is now a transformational coach, keynote speaker, twice an author and mother of four boys.

What matters most to me is feeling safe and secure. I am at my best and happiest when I am feeling love, and I am loving, when I'm laughing and delighting and when I'm having new experiences.

What drives me is learning new things and how I grow and evolve as a result. I come alive when I'm winning battles, defying the odds and achieving my impossible.

It's taken grit and determination to get this far. I've had to be strong. I've had to be resilient, and I've needed to think on my feet. It's also taken an unbelievable amount of courage. I've wanted to give up so many times, but each time I persevered. I put one foot in front of the other, and I just kept going.

My goal is to publish a bestselling book on Imposter Syndrome for people of colour; and now here I am inspiring and empowering people of colour around the world to become leaders of colour and help to bring more diversity, inclusion and equality into leadership.

EPILOGUE

Panic. Shortness of breath. A knot of anxiety in the pit of my stomach, and the familiar voice saying, "Caroline, you shouldn't be here!"

From backstage, I can hear the muffled mutterings of the audience as they prepare to take their seats. I can't see the room but I can tell it's filling up because the noise is getting louder and louder. The numbers expected for this talk far exceed any talk I've ever done before. The stage is bigger, the expectations – of the organiser, the audience and myself – seem so much higher. The irony of my Imposter Syndrome surfacing just as I'm about to deliver a talk on Imposter Syndrome is never lost on me. On any other day, I'd find it funny. Not today.

"I'm a fraud."

"I don't deserve this success."

"Any minute now I'll be exposed."

My throat is dry and I realise I've been holding my breath. I reach for the glass of water beside me and take advantage of the privacy to drink. The AV man checking my mic notices my hand shaking and smiles. "I can't wait to hear your talk. I hear it's amazing". He thinks he is helping. He isn't.

"My name is Caroline Flanagan."

The crowd settles. The lights begin to dim. The sound of my name through the microphone sends a bolt of adrenaline through my body. The event host is introducing me, reeling off a list of achievements that are both familiar and unrecognisable at the same time. My brain tries to reconcile the words that I'm hearing with the way I am feeling. It fails.

The room fills with the sound of people clapping and I realise it's time. The knot in my stomach tightens and for a minute the fear is so acute I can't move.

I want to run, but I don't. I know these thoughts and fears too well. And I know exactly what I need to do.

"My name is Caroline Flanagan."

The words flash up on a screen inside my brain and at the same time, I hear them whispered by my inner voice. They are all the words I need. I don't need to recite my whole Imposter Speech. I can already feel it in my body: where I am, why I am here, how I got here, and where I'm going. I feel a surge of courage. I know exactly what I'm here to do.

With a deep inhale I step boldly onto the stage and into the spotlight. The light is so bright it prevents me from seeing the audience, but that doesn't matter. I know you're there – a sea of colourful faces. An audience of high achievers. A room full of colour, proud to identify yourselves as imposters.

I smile. And then I begin.

WHAT WILL YOU DO?

*"Imposter – (1) a person who, through some
combination of ambition, luck, hard graft and
resilience, gains entry into a system designed to
exclude or alienate them; (2) a statistical anomaly
(3) the first and only one of its kind."*

- CAROLINE FLANAGAN

Everything we have done so far has been leading and
building to this point. Now the time has come for you to
step out into the world and see what you can do – knowing that it's hard and that the odds are against you, but
knowing that you are already everything you need. You've
got this. You are an imposter.

*"Give me a place to stand and I will
I move the Earth[19]"*

So said Archimedes, the Greek astronomer, physicist and
mathematician, who was regarded as one of the leading
classical scientists. I don't know how this quote winged its
way down through the centuries to land on the desk of

an 11-year-old black girl in an all-white school, struggling to make sense of her place in the world. But the moment that I read those words, they changed me. From that day, I understood that I didn't need to be given the Earth. All I needed was the opportunity, and the right tool, and I could do anything.

Wherever you are, whatever stage or level you are at, as a high-potential person of colour you have the opportunity. Now that you have your Imposter Speech, you also have the tool. You have everything you need. So, what will you do?

Who are you?

Where are you?

Why are you here?

How did you get here?

Where are you going?

There's no one like you. No one with your experience, your background, your values or your purpose. No one has had to work like you, struggle like you in quite the same way as you, against the odds like you. You're an imposter. What will you do?

You're a person of colour who is striving to succeed in a white world. Will you be a helpless victim waiting and hoping for the system to change? Will you be a powerless bystander waiting for the confidence to step up? Who will you be? What will you do?

I know what you'll do.

You'll be the first.

When you see there's no one who looks like you, you'll be the first.

When you're reminded the rules weren't made for you, you'll be the first.

When they say there's no room for you, or look straight through you, you'll be the first.

You have a place to stand. I've offered you a lever.

What will you do?

Are you still unsure of your power? Do you need my help?

If you're still unsure of your power or you'd like some help with your speech, visit **carolineflanagan.com/imposter-speech** for details of the Be The First group coaching programme.

Is your Imposter Speech already working for you?

If you've been using your Imposter Speech and getting positive results, I'd love to hear from you. Send me your feedback via:

✉ EMAIL: CAROLINE@CAROLINEFLANAGAN.COM

📷 INSTAGRAM: CAROLINE_FLANAGAN_

f FACEBOOK: CAROLINE.FLANAGAN.12

in LINKEDIN: CAROLINE FLANAGAN

DISCOVER MORE

🎙 THE CAROLINE FLANAGAN PODCAST

🏠 WWW.CAROLINEFLANAGAN.COM/IMPOSTERSPEECH

THANK YOU

To my mum: you have been fighting battles your whole life. Thank you for battling to send me off to boarding school at the age of six. That decision, and the challenges and opportunities that it forced upon me, is one for which I am deeply and eternally grateful.

To my Dad: thank you for how hard you worked to guide and protect me.

To my husband Paul: without your support, encouragement and unshakeable belief, this book would not be what it is. Thank you for being a pillar of strength to me, an inspiration to our boys and an incredible role model in the battle for greater equality.

To my editor Leila: thank you for your patience, persistence and absolute commitment to making this book the best it could be; for trawling through it so many times; for keeping your cool as you watched it grow, and for test driving the Imposter Speech and believing in its power. Meeting you at Antoinette's book launch as I contemplated the idea of the book, was a gift from the universe. There are no accidents!

To my brother Calvin: thank you for always being there and for giving me the courage to share my story. You are my role model, my mentor, my hero and my rock.

To my clients: thank you for trusting me with your goals, for being willing to be challenged and for showing up with the courage and determination to succeed. Coaching you is the most important and rewarding work I do.

To the amazing people in my professional network who are standing out and bringing value to the world – Lizzie Edwards (author of *Look Like The Leader You Are*), Antoinette Dale Henderson (author of *Gravitas* and *Power Up*), Deborah Henley (author of *Your Leadership Story*), Emma Stroud (founder of Laugh. Think. Play) and Patty Cruz-Fouchard (Founder of Organised and Simple) to name just a few: thank you for your support, inspiration, friendship and encouragement over the years.

To my incredible assistant Louise Cronk, my social saviour Karen Campbell (Karen Campbell Marketing) and my blog writer Jay Curtis: thank you for keeping the business afloat so I could concentrate on this book. And Susanna: thank you for keeping my family afloat!

To Rebecca Kaye, Penny Anderson, Claire Shields, Sally Bridgeland, Tara Thomas, Helen Muggeridge, Penny Brusarosco, Julie Green, Nicky Renwick - for always being there, and for bringing light and laughter to my world when I needed it most.

Last but not least, to the teachers who believed in me – Mr Moore, Mrs Hartshorne, Howard Norton, Vivien McCormick, Professor John Hatcher: you have touched and shaped my life in more ways than you can imagine. As brave and determined and resilient as I have been, I would not be who I am today without the guidance, encouragement and support you once gave me. Thank you.

(ENDNOTES)

1 Andrew Gilpin, "*Unstoppable People: How Ordinary People Achieve Extraordinary Things.*" (Random House Business Books, 1998).

2 Clance, Pauline R.; Imes, Suzanne A. (1978), "The Imposter Phenomenon in High Achieving Women: Dynamics and Therapeutic Intervention."

3 Gravois 2007; Harvey 1981.

4 "The Impostor Phenomenon," Sakulku and Alexander, *IJBS*, 2011

5 (Clance & Imes 1978) cited

6 Research by Sonnak and Towell (2001) found that high levels of impostor fears were associated with poor mental health – *The International Journal of Behavioural Science*, 2001.

7 The first Parker Review of ethnic diversity in FTSE was published in 2017, the Review made a series of recommendations and set a target for all FTSE 100 boards to have at least one director from an ethnic minority background by 2021 – "One by 2021".

8 I discovered this data from an article on the Barnardo's website in 2015 while exploring the "How did I get here?" part of my Imposter Speech (which you'll learn all about in Part III). At the time of going to press, the article had been removed, which is why it isn't cited here. But you'll find no end of research data on the plight of children who have a parent in prison and the likelihood of them becoming offenders themselves on the Barnardo's website: www.barnardos.org.uk

9 Secondment is like being on loan to one of the firm's clients to act as their in-house lawyer and reinforce the relationship between the firm and that client.

10   Build Africa is an African education charity working to end poverty through education. www.build-africa.org

11   https://www.npg.org.uk/whatson/bp-portrait-award-2018/exhibition/exhibitors-entries/a-throne-in-the-west

12   Enlist the help of a coach, attend an Imposter Workshop or sign up to the Imposter Speech Programme.

13   Bernadette Cooper is not her real name; however, it has the same lyrical tilt and punch as my client's actual name.

14   You'll find more information about these workshops at the back of this book.

15   This can be a couple of lines if it needs to be, but don't go mad. The shorter and punchier this is, the easier it will be to remember and use.

16   See the back of this book for details.

17   I am not counting my brief attempt at gas and air when I was in labour with Dylan, which I quickly gave up on when all it did was make me feel sick and slur my words.

18   If you are pregnant, don't do it. Or if you can't resist, don't say I didn't warn you.

19   The actual quote is, "Give me a lever long enough and a fulcrum on which to place it, and I shall move the world," however, this is the version that found its way to me.

APPENDIX

Values

The following is a list of words or phrases that illustrate values. As you contemplate this list remember that it is not the word itself that is important so much as the meaning that you attribute to it. You may even feel that combining two or three values together brings you closer to the real feeling of a value and what it means for you.

Achievement	Choice
Adventure	Excellence
Appreciation	Excitement
Autonomy	Flexibility
Balance	Freedom
Balance	Friendship
Beauty	Fun
Being authentic	Growth
Care	Health
Challenge	Honesty

Humour   Trust

Independence   Zest

Love

Loyalty

Nurturing

Openness

Order

Originality

Performance

Recognition

Respect

Reward

Risk Taking

Safety

Security

Spirituality

Stability

Tolerance

Printed in Great Britain
by Amazon